The Mind Control Machine

Artificial Intelligence, Algorithms, and the War for Human Attention

Introduction

In the modern world, humanity is surrounded by technology in ways that previous generations could never have imagined. Smartphones, social media platforms, search engines, and artificial intelligence systems have become deeply integrated into everyday life. From the moment people wake up in the morning to the moment they fall asleep at night, digital systems influence what they read, what they watch, what they buy, and even how they think. While technology has undeniably improved communication, productivity, and access to knowledge, it has also created an environment where human attention has become one of the most valuable and fiercely contested resources on Earth.

Behind every notification, recommendation, and trending topic lies a complex network of algorithms designed to capture and maintain attention. These systems are not random. They are carefully engineered through data science, behavioral psychology, and machine learning to understand human behavior and predict how people will respond to specific pieces of information. In essence, modern technology does not simply deliver content; it strategically selects and presents information in ways that keep users engaged for as long as possible.

The battle for human attention is now a defining feature of the digital economy. Technology companies compete aggressively to capture as much of the public's time and focus as possible because attention directly translates into revenue. Every second a user spends on a platform generates valuable data and increases opportunities for advertising. The longer people stay engaged, the more profitable the platform becomes. As a result, many of the world's most powerful companies have invested billions of dollars into understanding how the human mind works and how digital systems can influence behavior.

Artificial intelligence plays a central role in this new landscape. Unlike traditional software, modern AI systems are capable of learning from vast amounts of data and continuously improving their ability to predict human actions. These systems analyze patterns in online behavior—what people click on, what they search for, how long they watch a video, and which posts they interact with. Over time, AI builds detailed profiles that allow algorithms to anticipate what will capture a person's attention most effectively.

This process has led to the emergence of what many researchers describe as the "attention economy." In this economic model, human focus is treated as a commodity that can be measured, analyzed, and sold. Platforms compete not only for users but for the largest possible share of their mental bandwidth. The result is an environment where digital products are intentionally designed to be addictive, persuasive, and emotionally stimulating.

The consequences of this transformation extend far beyond entertainment or social networking. Algorithms now influence political discourse, shape public opinion, and determine which information spreads widely across society. News feeds prioritize certain stories while hiding others. Recommendation engines guide users toward specific videos, articles, and viewpoints. In many cases, individuals may not even realize how strongly these systems influence their perception of reality.

At the same time, advances in artificial intelligence have dramatically expanded the power of these technologies. Machine learning models can now analyze emotions, detect patterns in language, and identify psychological vulnerabilities. By combining these capabilities with massive datasets collected from billions of users, technology companies and other organizations possess unprecedented insight into human behavior. This knowledge can be used to improve services and personalize experiences, but it also raises profound ethical and societal questions.

The core issue is not technology itself but the way it is designed and deployed. Tools that can inform and empower people can also be used to manipulate, distract, or exploit them. When algorithms prioritize engagement above all else, they often amplify the most emotionally charged or controversial content. Anger, fear, outrage, and curiosity are powerful drivers of attention, and digital systems frequently reward content that triggers these emotions.

As a result, the modern information environment has become increasingly intense, fast-paced, and polarized. People are constantly exposed to streams of information competing for their attention, leaving little time for reflection or critical thinking. Many individuals feel overwhelmed by the sheer volume of content and struggle to distinguish reliable information from misleading narratives.

Understanding this new reality is essential for navigating the digital age. The systems shaping modern life are not neutral; they are products of economic incentives, technological design, and psychological insight. Recognizing how these systems operate allows individuals to become more aware of the forces influencing their thoughts and behaviors.

This book explores the mechanisms behind what can be described as the "mind control machine"—the vast network of artificial intelligence systems, algorithms, and digital platforms competing for human attention. It examines how these technologies work, why they are so effective at influencing behavior, and what their growing power means for society.

More importantly, it asks a crucial question: in a world where machines increasingly shape the flow of information and attention, how can human beings maintain autonomy, critical thinking, and freedom of choice? The answer to this question will define not only the future of technology but the future of human civilization itself.

Chapter 1

The Psychology of Human Attention

Human attention is one of the most powerful yet limited resources the brain possesses. At any given moment, the human mind is surrounded by an overwhelming amount of information, images, thoughts, and memories, and emotions all competing for recognition. Despite this constant flood of stimuli, the brain has a remarkable ability to focus selectively on specific details while ignoring others. This ability to concentrate on certain inputs while filtering out distractions is what psychologists call attention, and it is a fundamental mechanism that shapes how people perceive and understand the world.

Attention acts as the gateway to human experience. What individuals focus on determines what they learn, what they remember, and how they interpret reality. In essence, attention decides which parts of the external world enter the conscious mind. Without attention, the brain would be incapable of organizing information into meaningful patterns. Every decision, belief, and action begins with the simple act of paying attention to something.

However, attention is not an unlimited resource. The human brain evolved in an environment where information was relatively scarce and survival depended on quickly identifying threats, opportunities, and social cues. Early humans needed to focus on signals such as the movement of animals, changes in weather, or the expressions of other members of their group. Because of these evolutionary pressures, the brain developed mechanisms that prioritize information linked to survival, emotional significance, and novelty.

These biological tendencies still shape modern human behavior. The brain is naturally drawn to stimuli that appears urgent, surprising, or emotionally intense. Bright colors, sudden movements, loud sounds, and dramatic stories easily capture attention because they activate neural circuits that evolved to detect important changes in the environment. Similarly, emotionally charged content—such as fear, anger, curiosity, or excitement—triggers powerful responses in the brain's reward system.

One of the key components involved in attention is the dopamine-based reward system. Dopamine is a neurotransmitter that plays a central role in motivation and pleasure. When individuals encounter something interesting or rewarding, dopamine signals reinforce the behavior that led to that experience. This mechanism helps humans learn from positive outcomes and repeat behaviors that produce satisfaction or success.

In the modern digital environment, this reward system is constantly stimulated. Every notification, message, like, or new piece of content offers a small possibility of reward. The anticipation of something interesting—whether it is a social interaction, a surprising video, or breaking news—activates the brain's curiosity and motivates users to keep checking their devices. Over time, this cycle can create patterns of habitual attention that are difficult to break.

Another important aspect of human attention is its vulnerability to cognitive biases. Cognitive biases are systematic patterns in thinking that influence how people interpret information and make decisions. Because the brain must process enormous amounts of data quickly, it relies on shortcuts known as heuristics. These mental shortcuts allow individuals to make rapid judgments without carefully analyzing every detail.

While heuristics are efficient, they also create predictable vulnerabilities. For example, people tend to focus more on information that confirms their existing beliefs, a phenomenon known as confirmation bias. Similarly, dramatic or emotionally intense events often seem more common or important than they are, a bias known as the availability heuristic. These tendencies influence what people pay attention to and how they interpret what they see.

The limitations of attention also play a crucial role in shaping human perception. Psychological research shows that individuals can only concentrate deeply on a small number of tasks at the same time. Despite the popular belief in multitasking, the brain does not truly perform multiple complex tasks simultaneously. Instead, it rapidly switches between them, often reducing efficiency and increasing cognitive fatigue.

In today's digital world, this limitation is constantly tested. Modern technologies deliver an uninterrupted stream of notifications, advertisements, videos, and social interactions. Each of these elements competes for the same limited pool of mental resources. As a result, attention becomes fragmented, and individuals may find themselves constantly shifting focus from one stimulus to another.

Understanding the psychology of attention is essential for understanding the influence of modern technology. The systems that dominate the digital landscape—social media platforms, recommendation algorithms, and artificial intelligence tools—are built around these fundamental properties of the human brain. By analyzing behavioral patterns and psychological triggers, these technologies can predict what will capture attention and keep users engaged.

This does not mean that attention is entirely controlled by external forces. Humans still possess the capacity for awareness, reflection, and deliberate focus. However, the increasing sophistication of digital systems means that the competition for attention is more intense than ever before. Platforms are designed with a deep understanding of psychological principles, allowing them to exploit natural tendencies in ways that maximize engagement.

As the digital age continues to evolve, the psychology of attention will remain at the center of the struggle between human autonomy and technological influence. By understanding how attention works—its strengths, limitations, and vulnerabilities, individuals can begin to recognize the forces shaping their focus and decisions.

The chapters that follow will explore these dynamics in greater depth, examining how the mechanisms of human attention interact with algorithms, artificial intelligence, and the modern attention economy. In doing so, we can begin to understand why the battle for the human mind has become one of the most important challenges of the digital era.

How the Human Brain Processes Attention

Human attention is a complex cognitive process that allows the brain to select specific pieces of information from the vast stream of sensory input constantly flowing into our nervous system. Every second, our senses collect enormous amounts of data from the environment: sounds, images, textures, smells, and internal bodily signals. Yet the brain cannot consciously process all this information simultaneously. To function efficiently, it must filter, prioritize, and focus on what is most relevant at a given moment. Attention is the mechanism that enables this selection process.

At its core, attention functions as a mental spotlight, illuminating certain stimuli while leaving others in the background. When the brain directs attention toward a particular object or idea, neural activity related to that stimulus becomes stronger and more organized. At the same time, competing signals are suppressed or ignored. This selective amplification allows the brain to concentrate its limited cognitive resources on tasks that matter most.

The process of attention begins with sensory systems. Information from the external environment first enters the brain through specialized sensory organs such as the eyes and ears. These organs convert physical stimuli—light waves, sound vibrations, and chemical signals—into electrical impulses that travel through neural pathways to various regions of the brain. However, not all incoming signals receive equal treatment. Even at the earliest stages of perception, the brain begins filtering information.

One of the first key regions involved in this filtering process is the thalamus, a small but crucial structure located near the center of the brain. The thalamus acts as a relay station, directing sensory signals to appropriate areas of the cerebral cortex. It plays a significant role in determining which sensory inputs reach conscious awareness. When attention is directed toward a particular stimulus, the thalamus helps enhance signals related to that stimulus while reducing interference from less relevant inputs.

From the thalamus, information moves to specialized regions of the cerebral cortex, where higher-level processing occurs. Visual information, for example, is processed primarily in the occipital lobe at the back of the brain, while auditory signals are processed in the temporal lobes. These regions analyze the features of incoming stimuli—such as color, shape, pitch, and movement—before integrating them into coherent perceptions.

Attention is not controlled by a single brain region. Instead, it emerges from the coordinated activity of multiple neural networks working together. Among the most important of these networks are the frontal-parietal attention networks, which play a central role in directing and maintaining focus.

The prefrontal cortex, located in the front part of the brain, is particularly important for voluntary attention. This area is responsible for planning, decision-making, and goal-directed behavior. When a person intentionally focuses on tasks such as reading a book, solving a problem, or listening carefully to a conversation—the prefrontal cortex helps maintain that focus by guiding the brain's attentional resources toward relevant information.

Working alongside the prefrontal cortex is the parietal cortex, which helps determine where attention should be directed in space. The parietal regions of the brain are involved in spatial awareness and the orientation of attention toward objects or locations. For example, if someone hears a sudden sound behind them, the parietal cortex helps shift attention toward the source of that sound.

Together, the prefrontal and parietal cortices form a network that allows the brain to control attention in a deliberate and flexible way. This system enables individuals to concentrate on tasks that require sustained mental effort while ignoring distractions in the environment.

Another important system involved in attention is the salience network, which helps the brain detect important or unexpected stimuli. This network includes regions such as the anterior insula and the anterior cingulate cortex. Its function is to evaluate incoming information and determine whether it requires immediate attention.

When something surprising or emotionally significant occurs—such as a loud noise, a sudden movement, or a threatening signal—the salience network activates rapidly. This activation shifts attention away from ongoing activities and toward the new stimulus. From an evolutionary perspective, this mechanism was essential for survival because it allowed early humans to respond quickly to potential dangers.

In addition to voluntary attention and salience detection, the brain also relies on the default mode network, which becomes active during periods of rest, reflection, or mind-wandering. While this network is not directly responsible for focused attention, it plays an important role in internal thought processes such as memory recall, imagination, and self-reflection.

The interaction between these networks determines how attention shifts between external tasks and internal thoughts. For example, when someone is deeply focused on a task, the attention networks become highly active while the default mode network becomes less active. Conversely, when attention drifts and the mind begin to wander, activity in the default mode network increases.

Chemical signals in the brain also play a crucial role in regulating attention. Neurotransmitters—chemical messengers that transmit signals between neurons—help control alertness, focus, and motivation. Among these neurotransmitters, dopamine, norepinephrine, and acetylcholine are particularly important.

Dopamine is associated with reward and motivation. When the brain anticipates something pleasurable or meaningful, dopamine levels increase, encouraging the individual to pay attention to the stimulus that may produce the reward. This is one reason why novels or emotionally engaging content captures attention so easily.

Norepinephrine, another important neurotransmitter, helps regulate alertness and readiness to respond. It is released by the locus coeruleus, a small brainstem structure that acts as a central hub for attention-related signals. Increased norepinephrine activity enhances the brain's ability to detect and respond to important stimuli.

Acetylcholine plays a key role in sharpening sensory perception and supporting sustained attention. It helps strengthen the neural signals associated with focused tasks while suppressing irrelevant information.

Despite these sophisticated mechanisms, the brain's capacity for attention remains limited. Research in cognitive psychology suggests that individuals can actively maintain focus on only a small number of items at once. This limitation is partly due to the constraints of working memory, the system responsible for temporarily holding and manipulating information during cognitive tasks.

Working memory is closely linked to attention because it determines how much information can be actively processed at any given time. When working memory becomes overloaded, such as when a person attempts to multitask across several demanding activities, performance tends to decline. Errors increase, reaction times slow down, and mental fatigue develops more quickly.

Modern digital environments place constant pressure on these cognitive systems. Smartphones, social media platforms, and online services deliver continuous streams of notifications and updates designed to capture attention. Each alert or message has the potential to interrupt ongoing tasks and redirect focus elsewhere.

Frequent interruptions force the brain to repeatedly switch between different contexts, a process known as task switching. While task switching allows individuals to adapt to changing demands, it also imposes cognitive costs. Each time attention shifts from one task to another, the brain must disengage from the previous activity and reconfigure its neural resources to address the new one.

Over time, excessive task switching can reduce the brain's ability to sustain deep focus. This phenomenon has become increasingly common in the digital age, where individuals often divide their attention across multiple screens, applications, and streams of information.

Understanding how the brain processes attention reveals both the power and the vulnerability of the human mind. The neural systems responsible for attention evolved to help humans survive in complex environments, allowing them to identify important signals and respond effectively. However, these same systems can also be influenced by technologies designed to exploit natural psychological tendencies.

As artificial intelligence and algorithm-driven platforms continue to evolve, they increasingly rely on insights from neuroscience and behavioral psychology. By analyzing patterns in human attention, these systems can predict what will capture interest and hold focus most effectively.

The result is a digital landscape where attention has become a valuable commodity—one that companies, advertisers, and platforms compete aggressively to capture. To understand the broader implications of this transformation, it is essential to first understand the underlying biological mechanisms that govern how attention works.

The human brain remains an extraordinary organ capable of learning, adapting, and directing its focus intentionally. Yet in a world filled with competing stimuli and powerful technological influences, maintaining control over attention has become both more challenging and more important than ever before.

Cognitive Biases That Make Us Easy to Influence

Human beings often believe they make decisions based purely on logic, evidence, and rational thought. In reality, the human mind frequently relies on mental shortcuts that simplify complex information and allow people to make decisions quickly. These shortcuts, known as cognitive biases, are systematic patterns of thinking that shape how individuals interpret information and respond to situations. While cognitive biases help the brain operate efficiently, they also create predictable vulnerabilities that can make people easier to influence, persuade, or manipulate.

Cognitive biases arise because the human brain must process enormous amounts of information every moment. If people attempted to analyze every detail logically, decision-making would become slow and overwhelming. Instead, the brain relies on simplified rules that help it evaluate situations rapidly. These rules were shaped by evolutionary pressures in environments where quick decisions often meant the difference between survival and danger.

Although these shortcuts were useful in earlier stages of human development, they do not always function well in the modern information environment. Today, individuals are exposed to vast streams of news, advertising, social media content, and digital communication. In such an environment, cognitive biases can distort judgment and lead people to accept misleading information or persuasive messages without careful analysis.

One of the most influential cognitive biases is confirmation bias, the tendency to seek out and favor information that supports existing beliefs while ignoring or dismissing contradictory evidence. When people encounter information that aligns with their worldview, they tend to accept it quickly and with little skepticism. Conversely, when they encounter information that challenges their beliefs, they may scrutinize it more critically or reject it entirely.

Confirmation bias plays a major role in shaping how individuals interpret news, political messages, and social media content. People often gravitate toward sources that reinforce their existing opinions, creating environments where opposing perspectives are rarely encountered. Over time, this selective exposure strengthens beliefs and reduces openness to alternative viewpoints.

Another powerful bias is the availability heuristic, which influences how people estimate the likelihood of events. This bias occurs when individuals judge the probability of something based on how easily examples come to mind. Events that are vivid, dramatic, or widely reported tend to feel more common or more important than they actually are.

For example, intense media coverage of rare events—such as plane crashes or violent crimes—can lead people to overestimate their frequency. Because these events are memorable and emotionally striking, they occupy a disproportionate amount of mental attention. As a result, individuals may make decisions based on perceived risks rather than actual statistical probabilities.

The anchoring effect is another cognitive bias that influences decision-making. Anchoring occurs when people rely heavily on the first piece of information they encounter when making judgments. This initial reference point becomes the "anchor," and subsequent decisions are influenced by it, even if the anchor is arbitrary or misleading.

In marketing and negotiation contexts, anchoring can have a powerful impact. For instance, when a high price is presented first, people often perceive lower prices as more reasonable by comparison. Even when individuals recognize that the initial figure is exaggerated, it can still shape their expectations and influence their final decision.

Closely related to anchoring is the framing effect, which occurs when the way information is presented changes how people interpret it. Humans tend to respond differently depending on whether a message emphasizes potential gains or potential losses. For example, people may react more strongly to a statement that emphasizes avoiding a loss than to one that highlights achieving a gain, even if the underlying information is identical.

This sensitivity to framing can influence choices in areas ranging from healthcare decisions to financial investments. By carefully selecting language and presentation, communicators can shape how audiences perceive risks, benefits, and outcomes.

Another bias that affects judgment is social proof, the tendency to assume that the actions or opinions of others provide reliable guidance about what is correct or desirable. Humans are social creatures, and throughout history, survival often depended on cooperation and group behavior. As a result, people naturally look to others for cues about how to behave.

In modern contexts, social proof appears in many forms. Online reviews, popularity indicators, trending topics, and follower counts all signal what others are paying attention to. When individuals see that a large number of people support a particular idea or product, they may feel more inclined to adopt the same view, even if they have not independently evaluated the evidence.

The authority bias is another powerful influence on human behavior. People tend to place greater trust in information provided by individuals perceived as experts, leaders, or authority figures. This bias reflects an adaptive tendency to rely on knowledgeable members of a group when making decisions.

While authority bias can help individuals learn from experts, it can also lead to uncritical acceptance of information. When a message is associated with a respected figure or institution, people may be less likely to question its accuracy. This effect can be amplified when authority figures communicate with confidence and clarity.

A related phenomenon is the halo effect, which occurs when a positive impression in one area leads individuals to assume positive qualities in other areas. For example, a person who appears confident, attractive, or successful may be perceived as more trustworthy or knowledgeable, even when those traits are unrelated to the topic being discussed.

The halo effect influences many aspects of social perception, including political leadership, advertising, and celebrity endorsements. When individuals associate a product, idea, or message with someone they admire, their favorable feelings toward that person can transfer to the associated message.

Another important cognitive bias is loss aversion, the tendency for people to prefer avoiding losses rather than acquiring equivalent gains. Psychological research has shown that losses often feel more painful than gains feel pleasurable. Because of this asymmetry, people are highly sensitive to situations that threaten something they already possess.

Loss aversion can influence financial decisions, consumer behavior, and political attitudes. Messages that emphasize potential losses—such as losing money, status, or opportunities—often trigger stronger reactions than those that emphasize potential benefits. Communicators who understand this bias can craft messages that motivate action by highlighting risks or threats.

In addition to these biases, the human mind is strongly influenced by emotional reasoning, the tendency to interpret situations based on emotional reactions rather than objective analysis. When individuals experience strong emotions such as fear, anger, excitement, or anxiety, their attention becomes focused on information that reinforces those feelings.

Emotionally charged messages are therefore more likely to capture attention and spread widely. Content that provokes strong reactions—whether positive or negative—can activate psychological mechanisms that encourage sharing and engagement. In digital environments, this dynamic often leads to the rapid spread of emotionally intense information.

Another factor that increases susceptibility to influence is cognitive overload. When individuals are presented with too much information or too many choices, their ability to evaluate options carefully becomes limited. In such situations, people are more likely to rely on heuristics, default options, or persuasive cues rather than conducting detailed analysis.

Modern digital platforms frequently create environments where cognitive overload is common. Continuous streams of news updates, advertisements, and social media posts compete for attention, leaving little time for reflection. Under these conditions, cognitive biases become even more influential in shaping perceptions and decisions.

The existence of cognitive biases does not mean that humans are incapable of rational thought. Rather, it highlights the complexity of the human mind and the challenges of processing information in a rapidly changing world. Awareness of these biases can help individuals recognize situations where their judgments may be influenced by psychological shortcuts.

Understanding cognitive biases is particularly important in the digital age, where communication technologies are designed to capture attention and shape behavior. Algorithms, advertising strategies, and persuasive messaging often rely on insights from psychology to make content more engaging and influential.

By recognizing the cognitive biases that shape perception and decision-making, individuals can become more mindful of how their attention and beliefs are formed. This awareness provides a critical foundation for navigating an environment where information flows continuously and influence operates in subtle but powerful ways.

Ultimately, cognitive biases reveal both the strengths and limitations of human cognition. They allow people to make rapid decisions and navigate complex situations, but they also create predictable patterns that can be exploited by those who understand them. Developing awareness of these patterns is an essential step toward maintaining autonomy and critical thinking in an increasingly interconnected world.

Dopamine, Reward Systems, and Digital Addiction

The human brain is equipped with powerful biological systems designed to motivate behavior, reinforce learning, and ensure survival. Among the most important of these systems is the reward system, a network of brain structures that helps individuals recognize pleasurable experiences and encourages them to repeat behaviors that lead to positive outcomes. At the center of this system lies a neurotransmitter known as dopamine, a chemical messenger that plays a critical role in motivation, anticipation, and reinforcement. While dopamine evolved to help humans pursue essential goals such as food, social bonding, and achievement, modern digital technologies have learned to engage this reward system in ways that can lead to excessive use and, in some cases, digital addiction.

Dopamine is often misunderstood as simply the "pleasure chemical." Dopamine is more accurately associated with anticipation and motivation rather than pleasure itself. When individuals encounter a stimulus that signals a potential reward, dopamine neurons in the brain become active. This activity encourages the individual to pursue the behavior associated with that reward. Once the reward is obtained, the brain records the experience and strengthens the neural pathways that led to the successful outcome. In this way, dopamine helps humans learn which actions are beneficial and should be repeated.

The brain's reward system is composed of several interconnected structures, including the ventral tegmental area (VTA), the nucleus accumbens, and the prefrontal cortex. When a person experiences something rewarding, dopamine-producing neurons in the ventral tegmental area release dopamine into the nucleus accumbens, a region often associated with feelings of motivation and reinforcement. This signal communicates that a particular action or stimulus is valuable, encouraging the brain to remember it and seek it again in the future.

Under normal circumstances, this system supports healthy behaviors such as learning new skills, forming relationships, and achieving goals. However, the reward system is also sensitive to stimuli that artificially amplifies dopamine signals. Substances such as drugs and behaviors such as gambling can produce unusually strong dopamine responses, which can lead to compulsive patterns of behavior. In the digital age, many technologies are designed in ways that activate similar mechanisms.

Modern digital platforms, particularly social media applications, video streaming services, and online games—are structured to provide frequent, unpredictable rewards. These rewards may take the form of likes, comments, notifications, new messages, or interesting content. Each of these signals carries the possibility of social recognition, novelty, or entertainment. Even though these rewards may seem minor, they are sufficient to trigger dopamine release in the brain.

One of the most powerful drivers of dopamine activity is uncertainty. Psychological research has shown that dopamine levels increase not only when a reward is received but also when there is a possibility of receiving a reward. This phenomenon is like what occurs in gambling environments. Slot machines, for example, are designed to deliver rewards unpredictably, creating a pattern known as variable reinforcement. Because players never know when the next reward will appear, they remain motivated to continue playing.

Many digital platforms use similar reinforcement patterns. When a user opens a social media application, they may encounter something amusing, surprising, or socially rewarding—but the outcome is never guaranteed. This unpredictability keeps users returning to the platform repeatedly, searching for the next satisfying experience. Each refresh of a news feed or check of notifications becomes a small experiment in anticipation.

Notifications play a particularly important role in stimulating the reward system. A notification signals that something new has occurred, perhaps a message from a friend, a reaction to a post, or an update from a platform. Because these signals often represent social interaction or recognition, they can trigger strong motivational responses. Even before a user reads the notification, the anticipation of what it might contain can activate dopamine pathways.

Over time, repeated exposure to these stimuli can create habitual patterns of behavior. The brain begins to associate specific cues—such as the sound of a notification or the visual icon of an application—with potential rewards. As a result, individuals may feel compelled to check their devices frequently, sometimes even when no new information is available.

Another factor contributing to digital addiction is the speed and convenience with which digital rewards can be obtained. In earlier stages of human history, many rewards required effort and patience. Obtaining food, building relationships, or achieving social status often involves long periods of work and cooperation. In contrast, digital environments can deliver stimulation almost instantly.

This rapid feedback loop makes digital interactions particularly effective at engaging the reward system. A user can scroll through dozens of posts, videos, or messages within minutes, each offering the possibility of novelty or entertainment. Because the brain responds strongly to new and surprising information, the continuous stream of content keeps attention engaged.

The design of many online platforms intentionally encourages prolonged engagement. Features such as infinite scrolling, autoplay videos, and personalized recommendations ensure that users rarely encounter a natural stopping point. Instead of reaching a clear conclusion, users are presented with another piece of content that might be even more interesting than the previous one.

Personalized algorithms further strengthen this cycle by analyzing user behavior and selecting content that is likely to generate strong reactions. By tracking which posts a person likes, shares, or watches for longer periods, these systems learn which topics, emotions, and styles capture attention most effectively. The result is a feedback loop where users receive increasingly tailored stimuli that maximizes engagement.

The prefrontal cortex, the brain region responsible for self-control and long-term planning, plays an important role in regulating impulses generated by the reward system. When functioning effectively, the prefrontal cortex can help individuals resist temptations and prioritize important tasks over immediate gratification. However, constant stimulation from digital platforms can place significant demands on this regulatory system.

Frequent interruptions and reward cues can weaken the ability to sustain focused attention. When individuals repeatedly switch between tasks—checking messages, browsing content, and responding to notifications—the brain's capacity for deep concentration may decline. Over time, people may find it more difficult to engage in activities that require sustained effort, such as reading complex material or solving challenging problems.

Digital addiction does not necessarily resemble traditional forms of addiction, but it shares several psychological features. Individuals may feel a strong urge to check their devices even when they intend to focus on other activities. They may experience discomfort or anxiety when separated from their phones or when unable to access the internet. In some cases, excessive digital use can interfere with sleep, productivity, and social relationships.

Researchers have also observed that excessive stimulation of the reward system can alter dopamine sensitivity. When the brain becomes accustomed to frequent bursts of stimulation, everyday activities may feel less engaging by comparison. This phenomenon, sometimes described as dopamine desensitization, can make it harder for individuals to find satisfaction in slower, less stimulating experiences.

Despite these challenges, it is important to recognize that digital technologies themselves are not inherently harmful. Many online tools provide valuable opportunities for communication, education, creativity, and collaboration. The issue arises when the design of digital systems prioritizes continuous engagement without considering the long-term effects on attention and well-being.

Understanding the relationship between dopamine, reward systems, and digital behavior is a crucial step toward developing healthier interactions with technology. By recognizing how digital environments activate motivational pathways in the brain, individuals can become more aware of the forces influencing their habits and choices.

Developing mindful technology involves creating boundaries that protect attention and mental balance. Strategies such as disabling unnecessary notifications, setting designated times for checking devices, and engaging in offline activities can help restore equilibrium within the brain's reward system.

Ultimately, the human brain evolved to pursue meaningful goals, build relationships, and explore the world. While digital platforms can offer valuable experience, maintaining control over attention ensures that technology remains a tool rather than a source of dependency. As society continues to navigate the digital era, understanding the biological foundations of motivation and reward will be essential for preserving both productivity and psychological well-being.

Why Humans Struggle to Resist Instant Gratification

One of the most persistent characteristics of human behavior is the tendency to prefer immediate rewards over larger rewards that may come later. This tendency, often described as instant gratification, plays a powerful role in shaping decisions, habits, and long-term outcomes. People frequently choose the satisfaction that is available now—even when waiting would produce greater benefits in the future. Whether it involves checking social media instead of completing important work, choosing unhealthy food instead of nutritious meals, or making impulsive purchases instead of saving money, the struggle between immediate pleasure and long-term benefit is deeply rooted in human psychology and biology.

The human brain did not evolve in an environment where long-term planning was always possible or necessary. For most of human history, survival depended on responding quickly to opportunities and threats in the surrounding environment. Food sources could be scarce, resources unpredictable, and dangers immediate. In such conditions, individuals who quickly took advantage of available rewards—such as food, shelter, or social cooperation—often had a greater chance of survival. As a result, the brain developed mechanisms that strongly favor rewards that are available in the present moment.

This evolutionary background helps explain why instant gratification feels so natural. The brain's reward system is designed to reinforce behaviors that produce quick positive outcomes. When a person experiences something pleasurable, the brain releases neurotransmitters such as dopamine, which strengthens the association between the behavior and the reward. Over time, these biological responses encourage individuals to repeat behaviors that provide immediate satisfaction.

However, modern life presents a very different environment from the one in which these neural systems evolved. Today, people are surrounded by countless opportunities for instant gratification, especially in digital environments. Smartphones, online shopping platforms, streaming services, and social media applications provide immediate access to entertainment, information, and social interaction. Because these rewards can be obtained with minimal effort, the brain receives frequent bursts of stimulation that reinforce the desire for instant pleasure.

Another important factor that contributes to instant gratification is the interaction between two major systems in the brain: the limbic system and the prefrontal cortex. The limbic system, which includes structures such as the amygdala and nucleus accumbens, is heavily involved in emotion, motivation, and reward processing. It responds quickly to stimuli that promise pleasure or relief from discomfort.

The prefrontal cortex, located in the front of the brain, is responsible for higher-level cognitive functions such as planning, decision-making, and self-control. This region allows individuals to evaluate long-term consequences and regulate impulses generated by the limbic system. When functioning effectively, the prefrontal cortex helps people delay gratification to achieve more valuable outcomes in the future.

The struggle between these two systems is central to human decision-making. The limbic system tends to prioritize immediate rewards, while the prefrontal cortex considers long-term goals and consequences. When the limbic system generates strong signals—such as the desire to check a phone notification or indulge in a tempting snack—the prefrontal cortex must exert effort to resist the impulse. This process requires mental energy and sustained attention.

Research in psychology has shown that delaying gratification can be difficult because the brain tends to discount the value of future rewards. This phenomenon is known as temporal discounting. In temporal discounting, people perceive rewards that occur in the future as less valuable than rewards that occur immediately, even if the future reward is objectively larger.

For example, when individuals are given the choice between receiving a small amount of money today or a larger amount of money in the future, many prefer the immediate reward. The future benefit may be greater, but the delay reduces its psychological value. This tendency reflects the brain's bias toward certainty and immediacy.

Another reason humans struggle with instant gratification is the role of uncertainty about the future. Future rewards often involve some degree of risk or unpredictability. Waiting for a benefit that may or may not occur can feel less appealing than accepting a guaranteed reward in the present moment. The brain tends to favor outcomes that are certain and immediately available.

Emotion also plays a significant role in the pursuit of instant gratification. When individuals experience stress, boredom, anxiety, or fatigue, the desire for quick relief becomes stronger. Activities that provide immediate pleasure—such as browsing social media, eating comfort food, or watching entertaining videos—can temporarily reduce negative emotions. As a result, people may turn to these activities as a form of emotional regulation.

In digital environments, this dynamic is particularly powerful. Online platforms are designed to provide continuous streams of content that can quickly shift a user's emotional state. A humorous video, an interesting article, or a message from a friend can provide a moment of satisfaction. Because these experiences are easy to access and repeat, they reinforce habits of seeking quick rewards.

Technology companies have learned to design digital experiences that align with the brain's preference for immediate feedback. Features such as notifications, likes, comments, and real-time updates create constant opportunities for small rewards. Each interaction offers the possibility of social recognition or new information, which can activate the brain's reward circuits.

This constant stimulation can make it increasingly difficult for individuals to engage in activities that require patience and sustained effort. Tasks such as reading complex material, studying for long periods, or developing new skills often provide rewards only after extended work. Compared to the rapid gratification offered by digital content, these activities may feel less appealing in the short term.

The concept of self-control is closely linked to the ability to resist instant gratification. Self-control involves regulating impulses and maintaining focus on long-term objectives. Psychologists have long studied the development of self-control in children and adults. One well-known experiment, often referred to as the marshmallow test, demonstrated that children who were able to delay gratification for a larger reward tended to achieve better outcomes later in life.

However, self-control is not a fixed trait. It can fluctuate depending on factors such as fatigue, stress, and environmental distractions. When individuals experience mental exhaustion or cognitive overload, the brain's ability to regulate impulses becomes weaker. In these situations, the limbic system's signals for immediate pleasure may become more difficult to resist.

Environmental cues also influence the struggle with instant gratification. The presence of tempting stimulus such as visible snacks, phone notifications, or advertisements—can trigger impulses even when individuals intend to focus on other tasks. Removing or reducing these cues can significantly improve the ability to maintain self-control.

Another factor that contributes to instant gratification is the speed of modern technology. Digital systems operate at a pace that far exceeds the natural rhythms of human cognition. Information can be accessed instantly, messages delivered within seconds, and purchases completed with a single click. This rapid feedback reinforces expectations for immediate results.

Over time, the brain may adapt to this environment by becoming less tolerant of delay. Activities that require waiting—such as long conversations, slow-paced reading, or careful problem-solving—may feel frustrated compared to the quick stimulation offered by digital media.

Despite these challenges, humans can strengthen their ability to delay gratification. Strategies such as setting clear goals, creating structured routines, and minimizing distractions can help the prefrontal cortex maintain control over impulsive tendencies. Developing awareness of the psychological forces that drive instant gratification is also an important step toward managing them.

Mindfulness practices, for example, encourage individuals to observe their impulses without immediately acting on them. By recognizing the temporary nature of cravings or distractions, people can create space for more deliberate decision-making. Similarly, breaking large goals into smaller achievable steps can provide intermediate rewards that maintain motivation over longer periods.

Understanding why humans struggle with instant gratification reveals important insights into both human nature and modern technology. The brain's reward system evolved to prioritize immediate opportunities for survival and well-being, but this same system can be overstimulated in environments filled with easily accessible rewards.

As digital platforms continue to evolve, the challenge of balancing immediate pleasure with long-term goals will become increasingly important. Individuals who learn to manage their attention and impulses will be better equipped to navigate a world where opportunities for instant gratification are always within reach.

Ultimately, resisting instant gratification is not about eliminating pleasure or avoiding technology altogether. Instead, it involves developing the ability to choose when immediate rewards are appropriate and when patience and discipline will lead to more meaningful outcomes. In an age of constant stimulation, this balance may be one of the most valuable skills a person can cultivate.

Chapter 2

The Birth of the Attention Economy

Throughout most of human history, economic systems have revolved around the production and exchange of physical goods. Agriculture, manufacturing, and trade dominated global markets, and wealth was measured largely by tangible resources such as land, raw materials, and labor. As societies evolved and industrialization spread across the world, economies gradually shifted toward services, information, and technology. In the digital age, however, a new and unusual resource has emerged as one of the most valuable commodities in the global marketplace: human attention.

The concept of the attention economy refers to a system in which human attention is treated as a scarce and asset that companies compete to capture and monetize. In an environment where information is abundant and easily accessible, the true challenge is no longer producing content but attracting and maintaining the attention of audiences. Every moment people spend watching a video, scrolling through social media, reading an article, or engaging with an application represents an opportunity for companies to generate revenue through advertising, data collection, and digital services.

The rise of the attention economy did not happen overnight. Its roots can be traced back to earlier forms of mass media such as newspapers, radio, and television. These industries relied heavily on advertising as a primary source of income. Media organizations produced content designed to attract large audiences, and advertisers paid for access to those audiences. The larger the audience, the more valuable the advertising space became.

In these earlier systems, attention was already an important economic resource, but it was limited by the structure of traditional media.

Television channels had fixed schedules, newspapers were published once a day, and radio broadcasts were constrained by time slots. The amount of content that people could consume was naturally restricted by these limitations.

The arrival of the internet dramatically changed this landscape. Digital technology removed many of the barriers that had previously constrained information distribution. Content could now be produced and shared instantly across the globe. Websites, blogs, online videos, and social media platforms created an environment where information could be generated at an unprecedented scale.

As the volume of available content increased, competition for attention increased. With millions of websites and digital platforms vying for the same audiences, simply producing information was no longer enough. Success depended on the ability to capture and retain the interest of users in an increasingly crowded digital environment.

Technology companies quickly recognized that attention could be transformed into a powerful economic engine. By offering free services such as search engines, social networking platforms, and messaging applications, companies were able to attract vast numbers of users. In exchange for these free services, users provided something extremely valuable: their time, focus, and behavioral data.

This exchange became the foundation of the modern attention economy. When individuals use digital platforms, they generate enormous amounts of data about their preferences, interests, and habits. Every click, search query, video view, and interaction provides information that companies can analyze. This data allows platforms to personalize content and advertisements in ways that increase engagement and maximize the time users spend on their services.

Advertising plays a central role in this system. Digital advertising has evolved far beyond traditional billboards or television commercials. Online advertisements can now be targeted at remarkable precision. Companies can display ads tailored to a user's age, location, interests, purchasing behavior, and browsing history. This level of targeting makes advertising more effective and more profitable, further increasing the value for capturing attention.

To maximize engagement, many digital platforms have adopted design strategies that encourage continuous interaction. Features such as infinite scrolling, autoplay videos, push notifications, and algorithmically curated feeds are designed to keep users engaged for extended periods. The longer individuals remain on a platform, the more opportunities there are to display advertisements and collect behavioral data.

Artificial intelligence and machine learning have accelerated the development of the attention economy. These technologies allow platforms to analyze massive datasets and identify patterns in user behavior. By understanding what types of content people are most likely to engage with, algorithms can deliver highly personalized recommendations that maintain user interest.

However, the growth of the attention economy has also raised important questions about its broader impact on society. When companies compete intensely for human attention, they may prioritize engagement above all other considerations. Content that provokes strong emotional reactions—such as outrage, fear, or excitement—often spreads more rapidly and attracts more interaction. As a result, digital platforms may inadvertently amplify sensational or polarizing material.

The competition for attention can also influence how information is presented and consumed. News stories may be framed in ways that maximize clicks rather than provide balanced analysis. Social media platforms may promote content that generates strong engagement, even if it contributes to misinformation or social division.

At the same time, the attention economy has created opportunities for communication and creativity on a scale never seen before. Individuals can share ideas, build communities, and access knowledge from around the world. Entrepreneurs, educators, and creators can reach global audiences without the traditional barriers of publishing or broadcasting.

Understanding the birth of the attention economy is essential for understanding the digital world we live in today. The technologies that shape modern communication are deeply connected to economic incentives that reward engagement and influence. As attention becomes an increasingly valuable resource, the systems designed to capture it will continue to evolve.

The chapters that follow will explore how algorithms, artificial intelligence, and digital platforms compete in this complex landscape. By examining the forces that drive the attention economy, we can better understand how our focus is shaped—and why the battle for human attention has become one of the defining struggles of the modern age.

From Television to Social Media: The Evolution of Media Influence

The influence of media on society has undergone a profound transformation over the past century. What began as centralized communication through radio and television has gradually evolved into a complex, decentralized digital ecosystem dominated by social media platforms, algorithms, and user-generated content. This evolution has fundamentally reshaped how information spreads, how public opinion forms, and how individuals interact with media. The journey from television broadcasting to social media networks illustrates not only a technological transformation but also a shift in the mechanisms of influence that shape modern society.

In the early twentieth century, mass communication was largely controlled by traditional broadcast media. Radio was one of the first technologies capable of delivering information to large audiences simultaneously. Governments, news organizations, and entertainment companies quickly recognized its power to reach millions of listeners in real time. Radio broadcasts created a shared informational environment in which large populations could experience the same news events, speeches, and cultural programs together. During times of war or political crisis, radio became a powerful tool for shaping public perception and mobilizing national sentiment.

The introduction of television expanded the influence of broadcast media even further. By the mid-twentieth century, television had become the dominant source of news and entertainment in many parts of the world. Families gathered around television sets to watch nightly news broadcasts, popular entertainment programs, and major political events. Because television required expensive infrastructure and broadcasting licenses, only a limited number of networks controlled the flow of information. This centralized structure gave media organizations significant power to determine what stories were presented to the public and how those stories were framed.

Television's visual nature made it particularly effective at shaping public perception. Images and live footage created emotional connections that written or spoken messages alone could not achieve. Political campaigns quickly adapted to the new medium, understanding that visual presentation could influence voter perceptions. Candidates who appeared confident, charismatic, and relatable on television often gained advantages over those who struggled with the format. The famous 1960 presidential debate between John F. Kennedy and Richard Nixon demonstrated how television could shape political outcomes. Viewers who watched the debate on television tended to perceive Kennedy as more composed and persuasive, while radio listeners often judged the debate differently.

Advertising also flourished in the age of television. Businesses realized that television provided an unparalleled opportunity to reach large audiences and promote products on a massive scale. Commercials became a central part of television programming, and companies invested heavily in crafting persuasive messages designed to capture viewer attention. The economic model of television relied heavily on advertising revenue, which meant that attracting and maintaining large audiences became a top priority for broadcasters.

Despite its immense influence, television remained fundamentally a one-way communication system. Broadcasters produced content, and viewers consumed it. The audience had little opportunity to interact directly with the content or with the creators behind it. Although television shaped cultural trends and public discussions, the flow of information remained largely controlled by a relatively small number of media institutions.

The emergence of the internet in the late twentieth century began to disrupt this traditional model. Unlike television, the internet allowed information to move in multiple directions. Individuals could publish their own content through websites, blogs, and online forums, reaching audiences without relying on traditional media organizations. This shift marked the beginning of a more decentralized communication environment where influence was no longer limited to large broadcasting networks.

During the early years of the internet, online media still resembled traditional publishing in many ways. News organizations created digital versions of newspapers, and websites provided written articles, images, and videos. However, the interactive capabilities of the internet introduced new possibilities for engagement. Readers could comment on articles, participate in discussions, and share information across online communities. This interaction began to transform audiences from passive consumers into active participants in the media ecosystem.

The most dramatic transformation in media influence occurred with the rise of social media platforms in the early twenty-first century. Platforms such as Facebook, YouTube, Twitter, Instagram, and later TikTok introduced a fundamentally new model of communication. Instead of relying solely on professional journalists or media companies to produce content, social media allows ordinary individuals to create and share information with global audiences. This shift blurred the distinction between content producers and consumers.

Social media networks expanded rapidly because they offered something television never could: direct interaction between users. People could comment on posts, share content instantly, respond to events in real time, and build communities around shared interests. This interactive environment created a dynamic information landscape where ideas could spread quickly through networks of users.

The speed of communication increased dramatically as well. News events that once took hours or days to circulate through traditional media could now reach global audiences within minutes. A single video recorded on a smartphone could be shared across platforms and viewed by millions of people around the world. Viral content became a defining feature of social media, with certain posts, memes, or videos spreading rapidly through online communities.

Another important development in the evolution of media influence was the rise of algorithmic content distribution. Social media platforms generate enormous amounts of content every second, far more than any individual could possibly consume. To manage this volume, platforms rely on algorithms that analyse user behaviour and determine which posts are most likely to capture attention.

These algorithms track a wide range of signals, including likes, shares, comments, viewing time, and browsing patterns. By analysing this data, platforms create personalized feeds that display content tailored to each user's preferences and interests. As a result, no two users experience the exact same information environment.

Personalized algorithms have greatly increased the effectiveness of media influence. Instead of broadcasting the same message to everyone, digital platforms can deliver highly targeted content designed to appeal to specific individuals or demographic groups. This capability has transformed advertising, political communication, and marketing strategies.

At the same time, algorithmic personalization has introduced new challenges. Because algorithms prioritize content that generates engagement, they often promote material that evokes strong emotional reactions. Posts that trigger curiosity, excitement, anger, or outrage tend to receive more interaction and are therefore more likely to appear prominently in users' feeds. This dynamic can amplify sensational or controversial content, sometimes contributing to polarization and misinformation.

Social media has also altered the concept of authority in media. In the age of television, news organizations and professional journalists served as gatekeepers who determined which stories were presented to the public. In the digital era, information can spread widely even if it originates from individuals with little institutional credibility. While this democratization allows more voices to be heard, it also creates challenges for verifying the accuracy of information.

The evolution from television to social media represents a shift from centralized media control to a complex network of distributed influence. Traditional broadcasters once shaped public opinion through carefully curated programming but today influence often emerges from interactions among millions of users across digital platforms.

This transformation has created both opportunities and risks. Social media allows people to share ideas, build communities, and mobilize around important causes. At the same time, the rapid spread of information can make it difficult to distinguish between reliable sources and misleading narratives.

As technology continues to advance, the mechanisms of media influence will likely evolve even further. Artificial intelligence, immersive media, and emerging digital platforms may introduce new forms of communication that further reshape how attention and information circulate through society.

Understanding the evolution of media influence—from the centralized power of television broadcasting to the dynamic networks of social media—is essential for navigating the modern information landscape. The tools that shape communication today are not merely technological innovations; they are powerful systems that influence how individuals perceive reality, form opinions, and interact with the world around them.

Why Platforms Compete for Your Time and Focus

In the digital age, human attention has become one of the most valuable resources in the global economy. Unlike traditional resources such as oil, land, or raw materials, attention is intangible, yet it holds immense economic value. Every moment a person spends browsing a website, scrolling through social media, watching a video, or interacting with an application represents an opportunity for companies to generate revenue. Because attention is limited everyone has only a finite number of hours in a day—digital platforms compete intensely to capture and retain as much of that time as possible.

The competition for attention arises from the economic structure that supports most online services. Many digital platforms offer their products free of charge. Social networks, search engines, video platforms, and messaging applications rarely require users to pay directly for access. Instead, these platforms generate revenue primarily through advertising and data-driven marketing. In this model, the user is not the customer but rather the source of valuable attention and behavioural data that advertisers are willing to pay for.

When individuals use digital platforms, they generate enormous amounts of information about their interests, preferences, and habits. Every search query, click, like, comment, and viewing choice contributes to a detailed behavioural profile. Companies analyse this data to understand what captures a user's interest and how long they remain engaged with certain types of content. The more time a person spends on a platform, the more data that platform can collect and the more advertising opportunities it can create.

Advertising revenue is closely tied to engagement. Advertisers prefer to place their messages where they are most likely to be seen and remembered. Platforms that can hold user attention for extended periods become highly attractive advertising environments. As a result, companies design their digital products in ways that maximize the time users spend interacting with them.

This economic incentive explains why many platforms measure success in terms of engagement metrics. These metrics include time spent on the platform, number of interactions, frequency of visits, and content consumption patterns. The longer users remain engaged, the more valuable the platform becomes from a commercial perspective.

Another reason platforms compete for attention is the network effect, a phenomenon in which the value of a service increases as more people uses it. Social media platforms rely heavily on this dynamic. When a platform attracts a large user base, it becomes more appealing to new users because it offers greater opportunities for social interaction. The presence of friends, family members, colleagues, and communities encourages individuals to remain active on the platform.

Network effects can create powerful feedback loops. As more users join a platform, more content is generated, which in turn attracts additional users. This cycle strengthens the platform's influence and increases its ability to dominate the digital landscape. Companies therefore have strong incentives to keep users engaged and prevent them from migrating to competing services.

The competition for attention is also intensified by the sheer abundance of digital content. The internet hosts billions of websites, videos, articles, and social media posts. Every day, enormous volumes of new information are uploaded and shared across digital platforms. In such an environment, capturing user attention becomes increasingly difficult.

To stand out in this crowded landscape, platforms invest heavily in technologies that enhance engagement. Artificial intelligence and machine learning systems analyze user behavior in real time, identifying patterns that reveal what types of content people find most interesting. These insights allow platforms to tailor content recommendations with remarkable precision.

Recommendation algorithms play a crucial role in maintaining user attention. By presenting content that aligns closely with a user's preferences, platforms reduce the likelihood that the user will become bored or disengaged. For example, video streaming services often recommend additional videos based on viewing history, while social media platforms prioritize posts that are likely to generate interaction.

These recommendation systems create personalized information environments where each user sees a unique combination of content. This personalization increases the relevance of what appears on the screen, making it more likely that users will continue scrolling, watching, or interacting.

Design features within digital platforms also contribute to the competition for attention. Many applications incorporate elements that encourage continuous engagement. Infinite scrolling, for example, removes the need to click between pages, allowing users to consume content endlessly. Autoplay functions automatically begin the next video or episode without requiring user input, extending viewing sessions.

Notifications serve as another powerful tool for capturing attention. Push notifications alert users to new messages, comments, or updates, prompting them to return to the platform even when they are engaged in other activities. Because these notifications often signal social interaction or new information, they can trigger curiosity and anticipation.

The psychological mechanisms behind these features are well understood. Humans are naturally drawn to novelty, social recognition, and emotionally engaging content. Platforms leverage these tendencies to keep users interested. When people receive likes, comments, or shares on their posts, they experience small bursts of satisfaction that reinforce the desire to continue participating.

Competition among platforms further intensifies this dynamic. Digital companies operate in an environment where switching costs are relatively low. Users can easily download new applications, create accounts on different platforms, and explore alternative services. Because of this flexibility, platforms must work continuously to maintain user loyalty.

If a platform fails to provide engaging content or appealing features, users may quickly migrate to competitors that offer more stimulating experiences. As a result, companies constantly experiment with new tools, interface designs, and content strategies to keep users engaged.

The global nature of the internet also means that platforms compete across international boundaries. A user's attention is not limited to services provided within a single country. Instead, digital platforms from around the world compete simultaneously for the same pool of users. This global competition encourages rapid innovation but also increases pressure to capture attention quickly.

The race for attention has significant implications for how information is presented and consumed. Because engagement metrics often prioritize content that generates strong reactions, emotionally charged material tends to receive greater visibility. Posts that provoke excitement, humour, anger, or controversy often spread more rapidly than neutral or nuanced information.

This dynamic can influence the types of stories and messages that dominate digital platforms. Content creators, marketers, and media organizations often tailor their material to attract attention in environments where competition is intense. Headlines may become more sensational, visuals more dramatic, and narratives more emotionally compelling.

While this competition can stimulate creativity and innovation, it can also create challenges. When platforms prioritize engagement above all else, there is a risk that accuracy, balance, or thoughtful analysis may receive less attention than content designed purely to capture interest.

Another important factor in the competition for attention is the relationship between attention and data. The longer users remain on a platform, the more data companies can collect about their behaviour. This data is extremely valuable because it allows companies to refine algorithms, improve advertising targeting, and develop new products.

Data-driven insights help platforms understand how users interact with content and what features encourage prolonged engagement. Companies use these insights to refine their strategies, creating increasingly sophisticated systems for capturing and retaining attention.

However, the competition for attention also raises broader questions about the role of technology in everyday life. When digital platforms are designed to maximize engagement, users may find themselves spending more time online than they originally intended. Frequent interruptions, constant notifications, and endless streams of content can fragment attention and reduce the time available for other activities.

Understanding why platforms compete so aggressively for attention helps reveal the underlying incentives that shape the digital environment. The struggle for time and focus is not merely a byproduct of technological progress; it is a direct consequence of economic models that reward engagement and data collection.

In this environment, attention becomes a scarce and valuable resource. Every moment spent online contributes to a complex ecosystem of advertising, data analysis, and algorithmic influence. Platforms therefore invest enormous effort into designing experiences that capture and maintain user focus.

Recognizing this competition allows individuals to better understand the forces influencing their digital habits. By becoming aware of how platforms operate and why they seek to hold attention, users can make more deliberate choices about how they engage with technology. In a world where countless systems compete for every second of focus, awareness and intentional use of attention may become one of the most important skills for navigating the digital age.

Advertising Models Built on Human Behaviour

Advertising has always been a central force in shaping how businesses communicate with consumers. From early newspaper advertisements to radio jingles and television commercials, companies have long sought effective ways to influence purchasing decisions and promote their products. However, the digital era has transformed advertising into a far more sophisticated system. Modern advertising models are no longer based solely on reaching large audiences; they are increasingly built on detailed insights into human behavior, psychology, and data patterns. By understanding how people think, feel, and interact with digital platforms, advertisers can deliver messages with unprecedented precision and effectiveness.

In traditional advertising systems, companies relied on broad assumptions about audience demographics. Advertisements placed in newspapers, television programs, or magazines were designed to reach general categories of viewers such as families, young adults, or professionals. Although these strategies could reach large numbers of people, they often lacked accuracy in targeting specific individuals who were most likely to purchase a product.

The digital revolution fundamentally changed this model. The internet made it possible to collect detailed information about how individuals behave online. Every interaction—such as clicking a link, watching a video, searching for information, or browsing products creates data that reveals patterns of interest and preference. This behavioral data has become the foundation of modern advertising systems.

One of the most important features of digital advertising is behavioral targeting. Behavioral targeting involves analyzing user activities across websites and applications to deliver advertisements that match individual interests. When a person visits online stores, reads articles, or watches videos about specific topics, those activities provide signals about their preferences. Advertising systems collect and analyze these signals to determine what products or services might appeal to that user.

For example, if someone frequently searches for travel destinations, visits airline websites, and watches travel-related videos, advertising algorithms may conclude that the individual is planning a trip. As a result, the user may begin seeing advertisements for airline tickets, hotels, or travel insurance. These ads are not random; they are based on patterns extracted from previous behavior.

Another powerful element of behavior-based advertising is retargeting, also known as remarketing. Retargeting occurs when advertisements follow users after they have shown interest in a product or service. For instance, if a person visits an online store and looks at a specific pair of shoes but leaves without making a purchase, advertisements for that same product may appear later social media or other websites. The goal of retargeting is to remind users of their previous interest and encourage them to complete the purchase.

This strategy works because human decision-making is often influenced by repeated exposure. Psychological research has demonstrated that people tend to develop positive associations with objects or ideas they encounter frequently. This phenomenon, known as the mere exposure effect, means that simply seeing a product multiple times can increase the likelihood of purchasing it.

Digital advertising platforms also rely heavily on predictive analytics to anticipate consumer behavior. Predictive models analyze vast amounts of data to identify patterns that indicate future actions. These models may consider factors such as browsing history, past purchases, geographic location, device usage, and even the time of day when users are most active.

By combining these variables, advertising systems can estimate the probability that a user will respond to a particular advertisement. Ads can then be prioritized and displayed based on the likelihood of engagement. This approach allows advertisers to allocate resources more efficiently and maximize the return on their marketing investments.

Social media platforms play a particularly significant role in behavior-driven advertising models. Unlike traditional websites, social media platforms encourage users to share personal information about their interests, relationships, and activities. This information provides advertisers with detailed insights into consumer preferences.

Platforms such as Facebook, Instagram, and TikTok allow advertisers to target audiences based on a wide range of characteristics, including age, gender, location, hobbies, lifestyle choices, and purchasing habits. Advertisers can create campaigns that reach individuals who fit highly specific profiles. For example, a company selling fitness equipment might target users who have expressed interest in health, exercise, or sports.

In addition to demographic targeting, social media advertising often relies on lookalike audiences. Lookalike audience technology identifies users who share characteristics with existing customers. By analyzing data from current buyers, algorithms can identify other users who exhibit similar behaviors or interests. Advertisements can then be delivered to these potential customers, increasing the chances of attracting new buyers.

Emotion also plays a critical role in modern advertising strategies. Behavioral research shows that people are more likely to respond to messages that evoke strong emotions such as excitement, happiness, curiosity, or urgency. Digital advertising campaigns frequently incorporate emotionally engaging visuals, storytelling elements, and persuasive language designed to capture attention quickly.

For example, advertisements may emphasize limited time offers, exclusive deals, or special discounts to create a sense of urgency. When consumers feel that an opportunity might disappear soon, they may be more likely to act quickly rather than delaying the decision.

Another behavioral factor that advertisers exploit is social influence. Humans are naturally influenced by the opinions and behaviors of others. Online advertising often incorporates elements such as customer reviews, ratings, testimonials, and popularity indicators. When consumers see that a product is widely liked or frequently purchased, they may feel more confident in their decision to buy it.

Influencer marketing represents a modern extension of this principle. Influencers are individuals with large followings on social media platforms who promote products or services to their audiences. Because followers often trust the influencer's opinions or lifestyle, their recommendations can have a strong impact on purchasing behavior.

The integration of artificial intelligence has further enhanced the sophistication of advertising models. Machine learning algorithms continuously analyze user interactions to refine targeting strategies and optimize advertisement delivery. These systems can test multiple variations of advertisements, adjusting images, text, and placement to determine which version performs best.

This process, known as A/B testing, allows advertisers to improve their campaigns based on real-time data. If one version of an advertisement generates more clicks or conversions than another, the system can automatically prioritize the more effective version.

Another important aspect of modern advertising models is real-time bidding. When a user opens a webpage or social media feed, an automated auction may occur in fractions of a second. Advertisers bid for the opportunity to display their advertisement to that specific user. The winning bid determines which advertisement appears on the screen.

Real-time bidding ensures that advertisements are matched with users who are most likely to respond to them. It also allows advertisers to adjust their spending dynamically based on the value of each potential impression.

Despite the remarkable efficiency of behavior-driven advertising, this system has raised significant ethical and privacy concerns. Because advertising models relieve heavily on personal data, users may not always be aware of how much information is being collected about their online activities. Data gathered from browsing behavior, location services, and device usage can reveal highly detailed insights into personal habits and preferences.

Critics argue that excessive data collection may compromise user privacy and create opportunities for manipulation. When advertisers possess detailed knowledge of consumer psychology and behavior, they may design messages that exploit vulnerabilities or encourage impulsive decisions.

Supporters of targeted advertising, however, emphasize its benefits. Personalized advertisements can help consumers discover products and services that match their interests, reducing the frustration of irrelevant marketing messages. Businesses can reach audiences more efficiently, and smaller companies can compete more effectively in digital marketplaces.

The reality of modern advertising lies somewhere between these perspectives. Behavioral advertising has undoubtedly increased the effectiveness of marketing, but it has also introduced complex questions about transparency, consent, and the balance between commercial interests and individual autonomy.

Understanding how advertising models are built on human behavior provides important insight into the digital environment. Every advertisement seen online is the result of sophisticated systems analyzing patterns of attention, emotion, and decision-making. These systems are designed not only to promote products but also to capture attention and influence choices.

As digital technology continues to evolve, advertising models will likely become even more advanced. Artificial intelligence, biometric data, and immersive technologies may enable advertisers to understand consumer behavior in ways that were unimaginable only a few decades ago.

In this evolving landscape, awareness becomes an essential tool for consumers. By recognizing how behavioral advertising operates, individuals can better understand why certain messages appear on their screens and how those messages are designed to influence their decisions. In a world where attention and behavior are closely monitored and analyzed, informed awareness may be the most powerful defense against manipulation.

Data as the Currency of the Digital Age

In the modern digital economy, data has emerged as one of the most valuable resources in the world. Just as oil fueled the industrial economy of the twentieth century, data now powers the technologies, businesses, and digital platforms that shape the twenty-first century. Governments, corporations, and technology companies increasingly view data as a strategic asset capable of generating enormous economic value. Every interaction in the digital environment—every search query, online purchase, social media post, and smartphone tap—creates information that can be collected, analyzed, and transformed into insights about human behavior.

The concept of data as the "currency" of the digital age reflects the idea that information about human behavior has become a form of economic exchange. Many digital services appear free to users. Search engines, social networks, video platforms, messaging apps, and email services rarely charge subscription fees for basic access. However, these services are not truly free. Instead of paying with money, users pay with their data, attention, and behavioral patterns. In return for convenient digital tools, individuals provide companies with valuable information about their preferences, habits, and daily activities.

Data is valuable because it enables organizations to understand patterns that would otherwise remain hidden. When millions or billions of people interact with digital systems, they generate enormous datasets that reveal trends about consumer behavior, social interactions, and cultural interests. By analyzing these datasets using advanced analytics and artificial intelligence, companies can predict what people are likely to do next. These predictions allow businesses to design more effective products, deliver targeted advertising, and make strategic decisions based on real-world behavior rather than guesswork.

One of the primary sources of digital data comes from online activity. When users browse the internet, they leave behind traces of their behavior. Websites can record which pages a visitor views, how long they stay on each page, and which links they click. Search engines track the queries people type into search bars, revealing what information they seek and what problems they want to solve. Social media platforms monitor interactions such as likes, comments, shares, and follows, creating detailed maps of social relationships and interests.

In addition to online activity, modern devices generate vast amounts of data through sensors and location services. Smartphones, wearable devices, and connected appliances collect information about physical movement, geographic location, and even health-related metrics. For example, fitness trackers measure steps, heart rate, and sleep patterns, while navigation applications record travel routes and commuting habits. Each of these data points contributes to a broader understanding of how individuals live and interact with their environments.

This continuous flow of information forms the foundation of what many analysts describe as the data economy. In this economy, companies collect data, refine it into meaningful insights, and then use those insights to generate revenue. Data can be used to improve user experiences, optimize product design, and enhance decision-making processes. However, one of the most profitable uses of data remains targeted advertising.

Targeted advertising relies on behavioral data to deliver personalized marketing messages to individuals who are most likely to respond. Instead of showing the same advertisement to everyone, digital advertising systems analyze user data to determine which ads should appear in each person's feed or search results. For example, someone who frequently searches for travel destinations may see advertisements for hotels or airline tickets, while someone interested in technology may receive ads for electronics or software.

The ability to match advertisements with individual preferences makes digital marketing significantly more effective than traditional advertising methods. Advertisers are willing to pay higher prices to reach audiences that have already demonstrated interest in their products or services. As a result, companies that control large amounts of user data can generate enormous revenue through advertising platforms.

Large technology companies have built their business models around this principle. Social media platforms, search engines, and online marketplaces rely heavily on user data to sustain their operations. The more users interact with these platforms, the more data is generated. This data strengthens the algorithms that power recommendation systems and advertising engines, creating a feedback loop where increased usage leads to more refined insights.

Artificial intelligence has further expanded the value of data. Machine learning algorithms require vast amounts of information to identify patterns and make predictions. The more data available, the more accurate these predictions become. For example, recommendation systems on streaming platforms analyze viewing habits to suggest movies or shows that users are likely to enjoy. Similarly, online retailers analyze purchasing histories to recommend products that match customer preferences.

Data-driven decision-making is not limited to commercial applications. Governments and public institutions also rely on data to inform policies and manage resources. Urban planners analyze traffic patterns to improve transportation systems, healthcare organizations study medical data to identify disease trends, and researchers use large datasets to study social behavior and environmental changes.

However, the rise of data as a central economic resource has also raised significant concerns about privacy and control. Many users are unaware of how much information is collected about their activities or how that information is used. Data collection often occurs automatically through cookies, tracking technologies, and background processes embedded within digital platforms.

Privacy advocates argue that excessive data collection may create risks for individuals if sensitive information is misused or exposed. Detailed datasets can reveal intimate aspects of people's lives, including their health conditions, financial status, and personal relationships. If such information falls into the wrong hands, it may be used for identity theft, surveillance, or manipulation.

The concentration of data within a small number of large technology companies has also raised questions about power and influence. Companies that control massive datasets possess significant advantages in developing advanced technologies and shaping digital markets. Because data fuels artificial intelligence systems, organizations with greater access to data often gain competitive advantages over smaller competitors.

Regulators in many countries have begun addressing these issues through new laws and policies designed to protect user privacy. Regulations such as the General Data Protection Regulation (GDPR) in Europe and similar frameworks in other regions aim to give individuals greater control over how their data is collected and used. These regulations require companies to be transparent about data practices and allow users to access, modify, or delete personal information stored in digital systems.

Despite these regulatory efforts, the role of data in the global economy continues to expand. Emerging technologies such as artificial intelligence, autonomous vehicles, smart cities, and the Internet of Things rely heavily on data to function effectively. As more devices become connected to the internet, the volume of data generated each day grows at an extraordinary pace.

Some analysts estimate that the world now produces quintillions of data daily, reflecting the vast scale of modern digital activity. This rapid growth suggests that data will remain a central driver of innovation and economic development for decades to come.

Understanding data as the currency of the digital age provides insight into how modern digital platforms operate. The information generated through everyday activities is not merely a byproduct of technology; it is an asset that fuels entire industries. Companies compete not only for user's attention but also for access to the behavioral data that attention produces.

For individuals, recognizing the value of personal data can encourage more thoughtful engagement with digital services. Awareness of how data is collected and used allows users to make informed decisions about privacy settings, platform usage, and the sharing of personal information.

As society continues to navigate the digital era, the role of data will remain central to economic systems, technological development, and social interactions. The challenge for the future will be finding a balance between harnessing the benefits of data-driven innovation and protecting the rights and autonomy of individuals whose data powers the digital world.

Chapter 3

Algorithms: The Hidden Architects of Reality

In the modern digital world, much of what people see, read, and experience online is not determined by chance. Behind every search result, social media feed, video recommendation, and advertisement lies a powerful set of mathematical instructions known as algorithms. These algorithms quietly organize the vast ocean of digital information and decide what content reaches users at any given moment. Although most people interact with digital platforms every day, relatively few fully understand how deeply algorithms shape their online experiences.

An algorithm, in its simplest form, is a set of step-by-step instructions designed to solve a problem or perform a specific task. Algorithms have existed for centuries in mathematics and computing, but the rise of the internet and artificial intelligence has dramatically expanded their role in everyday life. Today, algorithms process enormous amounts of data in real time, analyzing patterns in human behavior and making decisions about what information individuals are most likely to engage with.

As the amount of digital content continues to grow, algorithms have become essential tools for managing information. Every minute, millions of social media posts, videos, messages, and articles are created and shared across the internet. Without automated systems to organize this content, it would be nearly impossible for users to navigate the digital environment efficiently. Algorithms therefore act as filters, sorting through vast datasets and presenting users with content that appears most relevant to them.

However, algorithms do far more than simply organize information. By deciding which posts appear in a news feed, which videos are recommended next, or which search results appear at the top of a page, algorithms influence what people learn, believe, and discuss. In this sense, algorithms function as invisible editors that shape the digital reality experienced by billions of users.

Unlike traditional media, where human editors and journalists determined which stories would reach audiences, algorithm-driven platforms rely heavily on automated systems that analyze user behavior. These systems track signals such as clicks, likes, shares, comments, viewing time, and browsing patterns. By studying these signals, algorithms attempt to predict what types of content will capture a user's attention and keep them engaged.

This predictive capability has transformed the way information is distributed online. Instead of presenting the same content to every user, digital platforms create personalized experiences. Two individuals searching for the same topic or opening the same social media application may see entirely different information based on their previous interactions. The result is a highly customized digital environment tailored to each user's interests and habits.

Personalization offers many advantages. It helps users discover relevant information more quickly and reduces the overwhelming amount of content available online. For example, streaming services recommend movies based on past viewing habits, online stores suggest products aligned with shopping preferences, and news feeds prioritize stories that match a user's interests.

At the same time, algorithmic personalization introduces complex challenges. When algorithms consistently present content that aligns with a user's existing beliefs or preferences, individuals may become less exposed to diverse perspectives. Over time, this can contribute to the formation of information bubbles, where users encounter only a narrow range of viewpoints.

Another important feature of modern algorithms is their connection to the economic structure of digital platforms. Many online services generate revenue through advertising and engagement-based models. As a result, algorithms are often designed to maximize the time users spend interacting with content. Posts or videos that generate strong emotional reactions—such as excitement, curiosity, anger, or controversy—tend to produce higher engagement levels and may therefore be promoted more prominently by algorithmic systems.

This dynamic means that algorithms do not merely reflect user preferences; they can also amplify certain types of content more than others. Stories that provoke strong reactions may spread more rapidly, while nuanced or less emotionally engaging information may receive less visibility.

Artificial intelligence has further increased the power and complexity of algorithmic systems. Machine learning algorithms can analyze massive datasets and continuously improve their predictions based on new information. These systems adapt over time, refining their ability to identify patterns in user behavior and deliver increasingly targeted content.

Because these processes occur automatically and often invisibly, many users remain unaware of how strongly algorithms influence their digital experiences. Unlike traditional editorial decisions, which were often transparent and publicly debated, algorithmic decisions are embedded within complex software systems that operate behind the scenes.

As digital technologies continue to expand into areas such as finance, healthcare, education, and transportation, algorithms are beginning to shape decisions that extend beyond online content. Automated systems now help determine which job applicants receive interviews, which loans are approved, and which information is prioritized in public discussions.

Understanding algorithms is therefore essential for understanding the modern information environment. These systems act as powerful intermediaries between individuals and the vast digital networks they rely on every day. By organizing information, predicting behavior, and influencing attention, algorithms have become some of the most influential yet least visible forces in contemporary society.

This chapter explores how algorithms operate, how they learn from human behavior, and how they shape the digital reality experienced by billions of people around the world. By examining the hidden architecture of algorithmic systems, we can begin to understand the mechanisms that quietly guide attention, influence perception, and structure the flow of information in the digital age.

What Algorithms Actually Do Behind the Screen

In the modern digital world, algorithms operate silently behind nearly every digital service people use. Whether someone searches on the internet, scrolls through a social media feed, watches a video on a streaming platform, or shops online, algorithms are working continuously in the background to process information and determine what appears on the screen. Although these systems are largely invisible to users, they play a crucial role in shaping how digital environments function and how information is presented.

At their core, algorithms are sets of instructions designed to solve problems or complete tasks. In computing, an algorithm defines a sequence of logical steps that a computer follows to produce a specific outcome. These instructions may be simple or highly complex depending on the problem being addressed. In digital platforms, algorithms are used to sort information, analyze user behavior, identify patterns, and deliver personalized experiences.

One of the primary function's algorithms perform is organizing massive amounts of data. The internet contains an enormous volume of information, including billions of web pages, videos, images, and documents. Without automated systems to organize this information, users would struggle to find relevant content. Algorithms therefore act as powerful filtering mechanisms that search through vast datasets and rank results according to relevance.

Search engines provide a clear example of how algorithms perform this function. When a user enters a search query, the search engine's algorithm scans through an index of web pages to identify those most closely related to the requested topic. It then ranks these pages according to factors such as keyword relevance, website credibility, page structure, and user engagement. The highest-ranked results appear at the top of the search page because the algorithm predicts they are most likely to satisfy the user's request.

Algorithms also play a major role in personalizing digital experiences. Instead of showing the same content to every user, modern platforms tailor information based on individual preferences and behavior patterns. This personalization occurs through continuous monitoring of how users interact with content.

When someone browses a website, watches videos, or interacts with posts on social media, those actions generate behavioral data. Algorithms analyze this data to identify patterns in user interests. For example, if a person frequently watches cooking videos, the platform's algorithm may begin recommending more culinary content. Similarly, if someone regularly engages with technology news, the system may prioritize articles related to innovation and digital trends.

This process is powered by machine learning models that improve over time. Machine learning algorithms analyze past behavior to predict future preferences. The more data they receive, the more accurately they can anticipate what a user might want to see next. As a result, recommendation systems become increasingly effective at keeping users engaged with content that aligns with their interests.

Another important task algorithms perform is ranking and prioritizing content. On social media platforms, users may follow hundreds or even thousands of accounts. If all posts from these accounts were displayed in chronological order, it would be difficult for users to keep up with the constant stream of information. Algorithms therefore determine which posts appear most prominently in a user's feed.

These ranking systems analyze a variety of signals to decide which content should appear first. Signals may include how frequently users interact with certain accounts, how much engagement a post receives, how recently the content was published, and how long users spend viewing similar material. By combining these factors, algorithms estimate which posts are most likely to capture attention.

The goal of ranking algorithms is typically to maximize engagement. Content that receives high levels of interaction—such as likes, shares, and comments—may be promoted to larger audiences. Conversely, posts that generate little engagement may receive less visibility. This dynamic helps platforms maintain active user participation, but it also influences which types of content become widely seen.

Algorithms also perform the function of content recommendation, which has become central to many digital platforms. Streaming services, video platforms, music applications, and online stores rely heavily on recommendation systems to guide user choices. These systems analyze user behavior alongside patterns observed among millions of other users.

For example, if many viewers who watch one movie also watch another film, the platform may recommend the second film to users who enjoyed the first. This method, often called collaborative filtering, identifies relationships between user preferences and suggests content accordingly. Over time, recommendation algorithms become highly sophisticated in identifying patterns that link seemingly unrelated pieces of content.

In addition to personalization and recommendations, algorithms play a critical role in advertising placement. Digital advertising relies on algorithms to match advertisements with the audiences most likely to respond to them. When a user visits a website or opens an application, an automated process determines which advertisements should appear.

This process often involves real-time bidding systems where advertisers compete for the opportunity to display their message to a specific user. Algorithms analyze available data about the user—such as browsing history, location, and interests—to determine which advertisements are most relevant. Within milliseconds, the system selects the highest bidder and displays the advertisement.

By targeting advertisements more precisely, digital platforms increase the effectiveness of marketing campaigns while generating higher revenue from advertisers. For businesses, this approach offers the advantage of reaching audiences that have already demonstrated interest in related products or services.

Algorithms are also responsible for detecting patterns and anomalies within digital systems. Many platforms use algorithms to monitor activity and identify suspicious behavior. For example, financial institutions rely on algorithms to detect fraudulent transactions by analyzing spending patterns. If a transaction deviates significantly from a user's typical behavior, the system may flag it for further investigation.

Similarly, social media platforms use algorithms to identify spam, automated accounts, or harmful content. Machine learning models can analyze text, images, and user interactions to determine whether content violates platform policies. Although these systems are not perfect, they play a crucial role in maintaining the safety and integrity of digital environments.

Another important role of algorithms is predictive analysis. Predictive algorithms analyze historical data to forecast future behavior or outcomes. In e-commerce, predictive models may estimate which products a user is likely to purchase. In video streaming platforms, predictive systems determine which videos users are most likely to watch next.

Predictive analytics enables companies to anticipate user needs and deliver content or services at precisely the right moment. For instance, music streaming platforms may suggest songs that match a user's listening habits, while online retailers may recommend products that complement previous purchases.

Despite their technical nature, algorithms ultimately reflect human choices and priorities. Engineers and developers design algorithms based on specific goals, such as improving search accuracy, maximizing engagement, or increasing advertising revenue. The criteria used to rank or recommend content are determined by these design decisions.

Because algorithms rely heavily on data, their effectiveness depends on the quality and diversity of the information they analyze. If the data used to train an algorithm contains biases or incomplete patterns, those biases may influence the system's output. As a result, algorithmic decision-making can sometimes produce unintended consequences.

Transparency has therefore become an important topic in discussions about algorithmic systems. Many users remain unaware of how algorithms influence the information they see online. Because these systems operate behind the scenes, their decision-making processes can appear mysterious or opaque.

As algorithms become more deeply integrated into everyday life, understanding their role becomes increasingly important. From search engines and social media feeds to recommendation systems and digital advertising networks, algorithms quietly shape the structure of the digital environment.

By organizing information, analyzing behavior, and predicting preferences, algorithms determine much of what appears on screens around the world. Although they function as technical tools, their influence extends far beyond computer systems. Algorithms have become powerful intermediaries that guide attention, shape perceptions, and influence the flow of information in the digital age.

Recognizing what algorithms do behind the screen helps reveal the mechanisms that drive modern technology. The digital experiences people encounter each day are not random collections of information, but carefully organized environments shaped by complex computational systems working continuously in the background.

Recommendation Systems and Personalized Content

Recommendation systems have become one of the most powerful technologies shaping the modern digital experience. Whenever users open a streaming service, scroll through social media, browse an online store, or search for videos, they are often presented with suggestions tailored specifically to their interests. These suggestions are not random. They are generated by sophisticated algorithms designed to analyze patterns in user behavior and predict what content individuals are most likely to enjoy or engage with. In this way, recommendation systems have become a central component of the digital ecosystem, influencing how people discover information, entertainment, and products.

At their core, recommendation systems are designed to solve a fundamental problem created by the abundance of digital content. The internet contains an enormous volume of information, far more than any individual could ever explore manually. Streaming platforms host millions of movies and television shows, online retailers offer vast catalogs of products, and social media platforms contain billions of posts. Without assistance, users would struggle to navigate this overwhelming landscape.

Recommendation systems act as intelligent guides through this complexity. By analyzing user behavior and preferences, these systems attempt to identify the content most relevant to everyone. Instead of requiring users to search through thousands of options, recommendation algorithms narrow the possibilities and present a curated selection that aligns with their interests.

The process begins with the collection of behavioral data. Every time a user interacts with a digital platform, that interaction generates information about their preferences. Viewing videos, liking posts, sharing an article, clicking a link, or purchasing a product all provide signals that algorithms can analyze. These signals form the foundation of user profiles that describe individual interests and habits.

Once these profiles are established, recommendation systems apply various analytical techniques to identify patterns within the data. One of the most common methods used is collaborative filtering. Collaborative filtering works by identifying similarities between users. If two users demonstrate similar behavior—such as watching the same types of movies or purchasing similar products—the system assumes they may also share additional preferences.

For example, if many users who enjoy a particular film also watch another movie, the recommendation system may suggest the second film to viewers who liked the first one. This approach relies on patterns across large groups of users to generate recommendations.

Another technique widely used in recommendation systems is content-based filtering. In this method, the system analyzes the characteristics of the content itself rather than relying solely on user behavior. For instance, a movie recommendation system might examine attributes such as genre, actors, director, and themes. If a user has watched several action movies featuring similar actors or story elements, the algorithm may recommend other films with comparable characteristics.

Content-based filtering focuses on the properties of items rather than similarities between users. This method is particularly useful when platforms need to recommend new content that has not yet been widely viewed by other users.

In many modern systems, collaborative filtering and content-based filtering are combined into hybrid recommendation systems. These hybrid models take advantage of both user behavior patterns and content characteristics, allowing platforms to generate more accurate and personal recommendations.

Machine learning plays a critical role in improving the performance of recommendation systems. Machine learning algorithms analyze large datasets to detect complex relationships that may not be immediately obvious. Over time, these algorithms learn from user interactions and refine their predictions. As users continue to engage with a platform, the system becomes better at understanding their preferences.

This adaptive learning process allows recommendation systems to evolve continuously. If a user begins exploring new topics or interests, the algorithm can adjust its recommendations accordingly. For example, if someone who typically watches comedy films begins viewing documentaries, the system may gradually introduce more documentary recommendations into their feed.

Recommendation systems are widely used across many types of digital platforms. Streaming services rely heavily on recommendation algorithms to suggest movies, television shows, and music that match user tastes. These recommendations help users discover new content and encourage longer viewing sessions.

E-commerce platforms also depend on recommendation systems to guide purchasing decisions. Online retailers analyze browsing history, past purchases, and product ratings to suggest items that customers may find appealing. These recommendations often appear as sections labeled "Customers who bought this also bought" or "Recommended for you." By presenting products aligned with user interests, retailers increase the likelihood of additional purchases.

Social media platforms use recommendation systems to determine which posts appear in users' feeds. Because users may follow hundreds of accounts, platforms rely on algorithms to prioritize the content most likely to generate engagement. Posts that align with a user's interests or that receive high interaction from other users may be promoted more prominently.

Video platforms such as YouTube rely heavily on recommendation systems to keep viewers engaged. After watching a video, users are presented with suggestions for related content that may capture their attention. These recommendations are often based on a combination of viewing history, engagement patterns, and similarities between videos.

The success of recommendation systems is closely linked to the concept of personalization. Personalization refers to the ability of digital platforms to tailor content to individual users. Instead of presenting identical information to everyone, platforms create unique experiences based on personal behavior.

Personalized content increases engagement because it aligns more closely with user interests. When people encounter material that resonates with their preferences, they are more likely to continue interacting with the platform. For companies, this increased engagement translates into greater advertising revenue and stronger user retention.

However, the widespread use of recommendation systems also raises important questions about their broader impact on society. One concern is the formation of filter bubbles, environments where users are exposed primarily to information that reinforces their existing beliefs and interests. When algorithms consistently prioritize content like what users have previously engaged with, individuals may encounter fewer perspectives that challenge their viewpoints.

This narrowing of information exposure can contribute to social polarization, particularly in areas such as politics and public discourse. If users repeatedly see content that confirms their opinions, they may become less aware of alternative perspectives or factual corrections.

Another concern involves the role of engagement-driven algorithms. Because many platforms measure success by user interaction, recommendation systems may prioritize content that generates strong emotional reactions. Posts that evoke excitement, curiosity, outrage, or fear often receive more engagement than neutral information. As a result, algorithms may amplify sensational or controversial material because it captures attention more effectively.

Despite these challenges, recommendation systems also provide significant benefits. They help users navigate the overwhelming volume of digital content and discover information that might otherwise remain hidden. For creators and businesses, recommendation systems offer opportunities to reach audiences who are genuinely interested in their work.

Artists, filmmakers, writers, and educators can benefit from recommendation algorithms that connect their content with receptive audiences. In this sense, recommendation systems can serve as powerful tools for discovery and innovation.

Transparency and ethical design are becoming increasingly important as recommendation technologies continue to evolve. Researchers and policymakers are exploring ways to ensure that algorithms operate fairly and responsibly. Some platforms are experimenting with features that allow users to understand why certain recommendations appear in their feeds.

Ultimately, recommendation systems represent a significant technological achievement that has transformed the way people interact with digital information. By analyzing patterns in human behavior and preferences, these systems help individuals navigate complex digital environments and discover content aligned with their interests.

At the same time, the influence of recommendation algorithms highlights the growing power of automated systems in shaping human attention. The suggestions that appear on screens are not neutral selections but the result of complex processes designed to guide behavior and maximize engagement.

Understanding how recommendation systems function allows individuals to become more aware of the forces shaping their digital experiences. As technology continues to evolve, the relationship between humans and algorithmic recommendations will remain a defining feature of life in the digital age.

How Platforms Learn Your Habits and Preferences

Modern digital platforms appear remarkably intuitive. Social media feeds seem to know what kind of posts will catch a user's attention, streaming services recommend movies that match personal taste, and online stores suggest products that feel surprisingly relevant. This sense that technology "understands" users is not accidental. It is the result of sophisticated systems designed to observe, analyze, and learn from human behavior. Through continuous data collection and advanced algorithms, platforms gradually build detailed profiles of individual habits and preferences, allowing them to predict what users are likely to want next.

The learning process begins with data collection. Every action a user performs on a digital platform creates a small piece of information that can be recorded and analyzed. These actions include clicking on links, watching videos, liking posts, commenting on content, searching for information, and making purchases. Even passive behaviors—such as how long someone pauses on a video or how quickly they scroll past a post—provide signals about interest levels.

Each of these signals contributes to a growing dataset that describes how a person interacts with digital content. While a single action may reveal little by itself, the accumulation of thousands or even millions of interactions over time allows platforms to identify patterns. These patterns become the foundation for understanding user preferences.

One of the most important sources of behavioral insight comes from engagement data. Engagement refers to the ways users interact with content on a platform. Likes, shares, comments, and viewing time all indicate how strongly a piece of content resonates with a user. If someone frequently interacts with posts related to technology, sports, or cooking, the platform's systems interpret this behavior as a sign of interest in those topics.

Engagement signals are particularly valuable because they reveal not only what users look at but also what they care about enough to respond to. Platforms analyze these signals to determine which types of content should appear more frequently in a user's feed.

Another crucial source of information comes from search behavior. Search queries reveal what people are actively seeking at specific moments. When users type words into search engines or search bars within platforms, they express their interests and intentions directly. For example, someone searching for "best hiking trails" or "camera reviews" provides clear evidence of their current interests.

Search data allows platforms to detect both short-term and long-term preferences. A single search may indicate temporary curiosity, while repeated searches about the same topic suggest a sustained interest. Over time, these search patterns contribute to a detailed understanding of user priorities and motivations.

Platforms also learn about users through content consumption patterns. The amount of time spent watching a video, reading an article, or listening to music can reveal more about preferences than simple clicks alone. For instance, if a user watches an entire documentary but stops a different video after only a few seconds, the system interprets this difference as a sign of stronger interest in the first topic.

Viewing duration, scrolling behavior, and completion rates all serve as indicators of engagement quality. By analyzing these signals, algorithms can distinguish between content that merely attracts curiosity and content that truly captures attention.

Location data provides another layer of insight into user habits. Smartphones and connected devices often share information about geographic location, allowing platforms to understand where users live, work, and travel. This information helps digital services deliver locally relevant content, such as nearby restaurants, events, or transportation options.

Location patterns can also reveal lifestyle habits. For example, regular visits to gyms, parks, or shopping districts may suggest interests related to fitness, outdoor activities, or retail. When combined with other behavioral signals, location data contributes to a more complete picture of user behavior.

Device usage patterns also play a role in how platforms learn about users. The type of device someone uses, the time of day they are most active, and the frequency with which they access certain applications all provide valuable information. A user who regularly streams music during morning commutes may receive different recommendations than someone who listens primarily late at night.

These patterns allow platforms to tailor experiences not only to user interests but also to their daily routines. Content may be scheduled or recommended based on when users are most likely to engage with it.

The process of learning from user behavior is made possible by machine learning algorithms. Machine learning systems analyze vast datasets to identify relationships between user actions and content characteristics. These systems do not rely solely on predefined rules; instead, they continuously adapt as new data becomes available.

For example, a streaming service may initially recommend content based on broad categories such as genre or popularity. However, as users watch more videos, the algorithm begins to detect subtle patterns in their viewing habits. It may be noticed that a user prefers films with certain themes, directors, or pacing styles. The system then adjusts future recommendations to reflect these discoveries.

Machine learning models often rely on predictive analysis. Predictive models examine past behavior to estimate what a user might do next. If someone frequently watches cooking tutorials and interacts with recipe posts, the system may predict that they will enjoy similar content in the future. As a result, the platform increases the likelihood that such content appears in their feed.

Predictive analysis is not limited to entertainment content. Online retailers use similar techniques to anticipate purchasing decisions. By analyzing browsing history, past purchases, and product reviews, algorithms can suggest items that align with a user's shopping habits.

Another powerful technique used by platforms is user segmentation. Segmentation involves grouping users into categories based on shared characteristics or behaviors. For example, users who frequently watch travel videos may belong to a "travel enthusiast" segment, while those who engage with fitness content may be classified as part of a "health and wellness" segment.

These segments allow platforms to deliver targeted recommendations and advertisements more efficiently. Instead of treating every user as unique, platforms identify clusters of similar users and tailor content to each group.

Platforms also learn through cross-platform data integration. Many technology companies operate multiple services that share information with each other. For instance, activity on a search engine may influence the advertisements displayed on a video platform owned by the same company. This integration allows platforms to build richer user profiles by combining data from multiple sources.

Over time, the accumulation of behavioral data results in highly detailed digital profiles. These profiles may include information about interests, hobbies, social connections, purchasing habits, and daily routines. Although users rarely see these profiles directly, they play a central role in shaping the content and advertisements delivered to everyone.

The ability of platforms to learn user preferences offers clear advantages. Personalized content can make digital experiences more efficient and enjoyable by reducing the effort required to find relevant information. Instead of searching through endless options, users receive suggestions tailored to their tastes.

However, this process also raises important concerns about privacy and autonomy. Because platforms continuously monitor behavior, users may not fully realize how much information is being collected about their activities. The data used to improve recommendations can also be used for targeted advertising and other commercial purposes.

Another concern involves the potential for behavioral reinforcement. When platforms consistently recommend content like what users have previously consumed, individuals may encounter fewer opportunities to explore new topics or perspectives. This can limit exposure to diverse information and reinforce existing preferences.

Despite these challenges, the learning systems behind digital platforms represent one of the most significant technological developments of the modern era. By analyzing vast amounts of behavioral data, platforms can understand patterns of human activity with remarkable accuracy.

These systems transform everyday actions into signals that reveal what people value, what captures their attention, and how their interests evolve over time. In doing so, they create digital environments that adapt continuously to user behavior.

Understanding how platforms learn habits and preferences is essential for recognizing the influence these systems have on daily life. The content appearing on screens is not simply random information but the product of complex learning processes that observe, analyze, and predict human behavior.

As digital technologies continue to advance, the ability of platforms to learn from user behavior will likely become even more sophisticated. Awareness of this process allows individuals to approach digital interactions more thoughtfully, recognizing how their habits shape the information they encounter in the digital world.

The Algorithmic Feedback Loop

In the modern digital environment, algorithms do far more than simply organize information. They actively shape how people interact with content and how that content spreads across platforms. One of the most powerful mechanisms through which this influence operates is known as the algorithmic feedback loop. This loop describes a cycle in which user behavior influences algorithmic decisions, and those algorithmic decisions, in turn, influence future user behavior. Over time, this continuous interaction between humans and algorithms creates patterns that can significantly shape perceptions, preferences, and even social dynamics.

At its most basic level, the algorithmic feedback loop begins with user interaction. Every action performed on a digital platform—such as clicking a link, liking a post, sharing a video, or watching content for a certain length of time—generates behavioral data. These actions signal to the platform's algorithm that a user found a particular piece of content interesting or engaging. The algorithm records these signals and incorporates them into its learning system.

Once this information is collected, the algorithm adjusts its future recommendations. If a user frequently engages with content about technology, sports, or political commentary, the system interprets these behaviors as indicators of interest. As a result, the algorithm begins to prioritize similar content in that user's feed. The goal is to present material that the user is most likely to interact with again.

The next stage of the feedback loop occurs when the user responds to the newly recommended content. Because the algorithm has selected material aligned with the user's previous interests, the probability of engagement increases. The user is more likely to click, watch, or react to the content because it matches their existing preferences. Each new interaction generates additional behavioral data, reinforcing the algorithm's assumptions about the user's interests.

This process creates a self-reinforcing cycle. The algorithm observes behavior, adjusts recommendations, observes new behavior, and refines its predictions again. Over time, the algorithm becomes increasingly confident about what types of content capture the user's attention. As the system becomes more accurate in its predictions, the recommendations become more narrowly tailored to the user's established preferences.

While this process can improve user experiences by delivering relevant content, it also has broader implications for how information is consumed and interpreted. Because algorithms tend to prioritize content that aligns with previous engagement patterns, users may encounter the same types of ideas or themes repeatedly. This repetition strengthens the feedback loop and reinforces existing interests or beliefs.

The algorithmic feedback loop is particularly visible on social media platforms. Social networks rely heavily on engagement-based algorithms to determine which posts appear prominently in a user's feed. When users interact with certain posts—such as liking political commentary, sharing humorous videos, or commenting on social issues, the algorithm interprets these interactions as signals of preference.

As a result, similar posts are promoted more frequently in that user's feed. Over time, the user may begin to see a higher concentration of content related to the same topics or viewpoints. Because these posts continue to generate engagement, the algorithm becomes even more confident that the user prefers them. The cycle continues, gradually shaping the overall information environment experienced by the user.

Video platforms also demonstrate the effects of algorithmic feedback loops. Recommendation systems often suggest videos based on previous viewing behavior. If a user watches several videos about a specific topic, the platform's algorithm will recommend additional content related to that subject. Because the user has already shown interest in the topic, they are more likely to watch the recommended videos as well.

Each viewing session provides the algorithm with additional data about what holds the user's attention. If certain videos are watched to completion while others are abandoned quickly, the system adjusts its recommendations accordingly. Over time, the algorithm becomes increasingly precise in delivering content that aligns with the user's viewing habits.

E-commerce platforms operate through similar feedback mechanisms. When customers browse or purchase certain types of products, the system records those actions and recommends similar items in the future. For instance, someone who purchases outdoor equipment may begin seeing more advertisements or product suggestions related to camping, hiking, or travel gear.

The algorithmic feedback loop is not limited to individual users; it can also influence collective behavior across large groups. When many users engage with a particular piece of content, algorithms may interpret this widespread interaction as a sign that the content is highly engaging or relevant. As a result, the platform may promote the content to an even larger audience.

This amplification can cause certain posts, videos, or ideas to spread rapidly across digital networks. Content that generates strong engagement signals—such as high numbers of likes, comments, or shares—often receives greater visibility. The more visibility the content receives, the more users interact with it, reinforcing the algorithm's decision to promote it further.

Because engagement signals often reflect emotional reactions, the algorithmic feedback loop can sometimes favor content that provokes strong emotions. Posts that trigger excitement, curiosity, anger, or controversy tend to generate higher levels of interaction than neutral or informational content. As a result, emotionally charged material may spread more quickly and widely through digital platforms.

Another consequence of algorithmic feedback loops is the formation of information bubbles. When users consistently interact with content that reflects their interests or beliefs, algorithms may gradually filter out content that falls outside those patterns. This filtering process can lead to environments where users encounter fewer perspectives that challenge their viewpoints.

Over time, individuals may become surrounded by content that reinforces their existing opinions. Because the algorithm interprets repeated engagement as a preference for similar material, it continues delivering content aligned with those patterns. This process strengthens the feedback loop and can make it more difficult for users to encounter diverse ideas.

The design of engagement-based algorithms is closely linked to the economic incentives of digital platforms. Many online services generate revenue through advertising, which depends heavily on user attention and interaction. The longer users remain engaged with content, the more advertisements they are likely to see. As a result, platforms often optimize algorithms to maximize engagement.

By promoting content that keeps users scrolling, watching, or interacting, platforms increase the time users spend on their services. This increased engagement generates more behavioral data and creates additional opportunities for advertising revenue. The algorithmic feedback loop therefore supports both user engagement and the economic goals of digital platforms.

However, the influence of algorithmic feedback loops has sparked growing discussion among researchers, policymakers, and technology experts. Some observers argue that these loops can unintentionally amplify misinformation, sensationalism, or polarization. Because algorithms prioritize engagement signals, they may promote content that captures attention without necessarily evaluating its accuracy or societal impact.

Others emphasize that algorithmic systems can also provide benefits when designed responsibly. Recommendation algorithms can help users discover educational resources, creative works, or meaningful communities that align with their interests. When balanced carefully, feedback loops can enhance the discovery of valuable content rather than simply reinforcing narrow patterns.

Addressing the challenges associated with algorithmic feedback loops requires a combination of technological design, transparency, and user awareness. Some platforms have begun experimenting with ways to introduce greater diversity into recommendation systems or to provide users with more control over their content feeds.

For individuals, understanding how algorithmic feedback loops operate can help foster more mindful digital behavior. Recognizing that each click, like, or share contributes to shaping future recommendations encourages users to engage thoughtfully with content. By exploring diverse topics and perspectives, individuals can influence algorithms to present a broader range of information.

The algorithmic feedback loop illustrates how deeply human behavior and machine learning systems are intertwined in the digital age. Algorithms learn from human actions, but they also guide future attention and engagement. This dynamic interaction creates powerful patterns that shape the flow of information across digital networks.

As algorithms continue to evolve and become more sophisticated, the feedback loops connecting technology and human behavior will likely grow even stronger. Understanding this relationship is essential for navigating a world where the information people see and the choices they make are increasingly influenced by systems designed to learn from their every interaction.

Chapter 4

Artificial Intelligence and Behavioural Prediction

In the digital age, artificial intelligence has become one of the most powerful tools for understanding and predicting human behavior. While earlier technologies could store and process information, modern AI systems can analyze enormous amounts of data, detect patterns within that data, and use those patterns to anticipate future actions. This capability has transformed how businesses operate, how digital platforms engage users, and how decisions are made across many sectors of society. Artificial intelligence is no longer simply a tool for automation; it has become a system capable of learning from human activity and forecasting what people are likely to do next.

Behavioral prediction lies at the heart of this transformation. Every digital interaction leaves behind traces of behavior—search queries, clicks, viewing choices, purchases, social interactions, and location patterns. When these traces are collected across millions or even billions of users, they form vast datasets that reveal consistent patterns in how people think, react, and make decisions. Artificial intelligence systems analyze these datasets to identify relationships between past behavior and future outcomes. By recognizing these patterns, AI can generate predictions about what individuals may want, what they may believe, and how they may respond to specific stimuli.

The ability to predict behavior has enormous value in the modern economy. Businesses seek to understand customer preferences so they can offer products and services that match consumer needs. Digital platforms aim to deliver content that users will find engaging in order to keep them active on their services. Advertisers attempt to reach audiences who are most likely to respond to marketing messages. Artificial intelligence enables all these objectives by transforming raw behavioral data into actionable insights.

One of the most significant developments in this field is the rise of machine learning, a branch of artificial intelligence that allows computer systems to improve their performance through experience. Instead of relying solely on fixed programming rules, machine learning models analyze data to discover patterns and relationships on their own. As these systems encounter more data, they refine their predictions and become increasingly accurate.

For example, a streaming platform may use machine learning to analyze viewing habits across millions of users. By examining which types of films are watched together, how long viewers watch certain genres, and which recommendations lead to further engagement, the system can predict what a specific user might want to watch next. Similar models are used in online retail to anticipate purchasing behavior and in social media platforms to predict which posts will generate the most interaction.

Artificial intelligence can also detect subtle behavioral signals that humans might overlook. Patterns of activities such as the time of day a person browses certain topics, the speed at which they scroll through content, or the sequence of links they follow—can reveal preferences and intentions. By combining many such signals, AI systems create detailed behavioral profiles that help guide future recommendations and decisions.

This predictive capability extends far beyond entertainment or advertising. Financial institutions use artificial intelligence to assess credit risk and detect fraudulent transactions. Healthcare organizations analyze patient data to predict disease outbreaks or identify individuals at risk of certain medical conditions. Transportation systems use AI models to anticipate traffic patterns and optimize routes. In each of these cases, the goal is to transform historical data into forecasts that help organizations respond more effectively to future events.

However, the increasing use of artificial intelligence for behavioral prediction also raises important questions about privacy, autonomy, and the balance of power between individuals and institutions. When algorithms can anticipate preferences and actions with high accuracy, they may influence decisions in ways that are not immediately visible to users. Recommendations, targeted advertisements, and personalized content can shape what people see and how they respond, potentially guiding behavior in subtle but significant ways.

Another important issue involves the quality and diversity of the data used to train AI systems. If the datasets used for machine learning contain biases or incomplete information, the resulting predictions may reflect those limitations. Because artificial intelligence learns from past patterns, it may unintentionally reinforce existing trends rather than encouraging new perspectives or opportunities.

Despite these challenges, artificial intelligence continues to advance rapidly. Improvements in computing power, data storage, and machine learning techniques are enabling systems to analyze behavior with unprecedented depth and speed. The predictions generated by these systems are becoming more accurate and more influential in shaping digital experiences.

Understanding artificial intelligence and behavioral prediction is therefore essential for understanding how modern digital platforms operate. The technologies that recommend products, suggest content, and guide online interactions are built upon complex models that learn continuously from human behavior. These systems observe patterns in the choices people make, interpret those patterns through advanced analytics, and use the results to anticipate future actions.

As society becomes increasingly interconnected through digital networks, the ability to predict behavior will continue to shape economic strategies, technological innovation, and social communication. Artificial intelligence has introduced a new dimension to the relationship between technology and human behavior—one in which machines not only respond to human actions but also anticipate them.

This chapter explores how artificial intelligence systems analyze behavioral data, how predictive models operate, and how these technologies influence decision-making in the digital world. By examining the mechanisms behind behavioral prediction, it becomes possible to understand how algorithms and artificial intelligence are transforming the ways individuals interact with technology and with each other in the modern era.

The Rise of Machine Learning Systems

Over the past few decades, one of the most transformative developments in technology has been the rise of machine learning systems. Machine learning, a branch of artificial intelligence, has changed how computers process information, make decisions, and interact with the world. Unlike traditional software programs that follow fixed instructions written by programmers, machine learning systems are designed to learn patterns from data and improve their performance over time. This ability to learn from experience has allowed computers to perform tasks that once required human judgment, such as recognizing images, understanding language, predicting behavior, and recommending content.

The concept of machine learning is not entirely new. Researchers began exploring the idea as early as the mid-twentieth century when scientists wondered whether computers could be designed to simulate aspects of human intelligence. Early pioneers in artificial intelligence believed that machines could be trained to recognize patterns if they were given enough examples to study. However, during those early years, the technology needed to make such systems practical did not yet exist. Computers lacked the processing power, storage capacity, and data availability required to train complex models.

The situation began to change in the late twentieth and early twenty-first centuries. Advances in computing technology dramatically increased the speed and power of computers. At the same time, the expansion of the internet and digital platforms created enormous quantities of data. These developments provided the raw materials that machine learning systems require to function effectively. As computing power and data availability grew, machine learning moved from a theoretical research field into a central component of modern technology.

At its core, machine learning involves training algorithms to recognize patterns within large datasets. A machine learning model begins with a dataset containing examples of a particular problem. The system analyzes these examples and identifies relationships between different variables. Over time, the model adjusts its internal parameters so that it can make accurate predictions when it encounters new data.

One of the most common forms of machine learning is supervised learning. In supervised learning, the algorithm is trained using labeled data. Each example in the dataset includes both the input information and the correct output. For instance, if a system is being trained to recognize images of cats and dogs, the training dataset will include thousands of images that are already labeled with the correct category. The algorithm studies these examples and learns to identify features that distinguish cats from dogs.

As the system processes more examples, it gradually becomes better at recognizing patterns associated with each category. Eventually, the trained model can analyze new images that it has never seen before and make predictions about whether they contain a cat or a dog. This learning process allows machines to perform tasks that would be difficult to program explicitly through traditional rule-based instructions.

Another important approach is unsupervised learning, where the algorithm is given data without labeled outcomes. Instead of learning from predefined answers, the system attempts to discover patterns or structures within the data on its own. For example, an unsupervised learning model might analyze customer purchasing behavior and group customers into segments based on similarities in their buying patterns.

Unsupervised learning is particularly useful for exploring large datasets where patterns are not immediately obvious. Businesses often use these models to identify hidden relationships within consumer data, allowing them to understand how different groups behave and how their preferences evolve over time.

A third important approach is reinforcement learning, which involves training a system through trial and error. In reinforcement learning, the algorithm interacts with an environment and receives feedback based on its actions. Positive outcomes are rewarded, while negative outcomes are penalized. Over time, the system learns strategies that maximize rewards.

Reinforcement learning has been used to train machines to play complex games, control robots, and optimize decision-making processes. Some of the most impressive demonstrations of artificial intelligence, such as machines defeating human champions in strategy games, have relied on reinforcement learning techniques.

The rise of machine learning has been closely connected to the development of neural networks, computational models inspired by the structure of the human brain. Neural networks consist of layers of interconnected nodes that process information and transmit signals to other nodes. Each connection carries weight that influences how strongly signals pass through the network.

During the training process, the neural network adjusts these weights in response to data. By refining these connections, the network learns to recognize patterns and produce increasingly accurate predictions. When neural networks contain many layers of interconnected nodes, the approach is known as deep learning.

Deep learning has played a major role in advancing fields such as image recognition, speech recognition, and natural language processing. For example, deep learning models enable voice assistants to understand spoken commands and allow translation systems to convert text from one language into another.

The success of machine learning systems is largely due to the availability of large-scale data. Modern digital platforms generate enormous amounts of information through user interactions. Every search query, video view, online purchase, and social media post contributes to a vast reservoir of behavioral data. Machine learning algorithms analyze this data to detect patterns that reveal how people behave and what they prefer.

In digital platforms, machine learning systems are often used to power recommendation engines. These systems analyze user behavior to suggest content that matches individual interests. Streaming services recommend movies based on viewing history, music platforms suggest songs aligned with listening habits, and online retailers recommend products based on browsing patterns.

These recommendation systems rely heavily on machine learning because they must adapt continuously as user preferences change. Each interaction provides new information that helps refine the system's predictions. Over time, the algorithm becomes increasingly accurate at anticipating what users are likely to engage with.

Machine learning has also transformed search engines. Instead of relying solely on keyword matching, modern search algorithms analyze context, user intent, and historical behavior. Machine learning models help determine which search results are most relevant to a particular query, improving the accuracy and usefulness of search results.

Another important application of machine learning is fraud detection. Financial institutions use machine learning models to analyze transaction patterns and identify unusual activity that may indicate fraud. Because these systems learn from historical data, they can detect subtle anomalies that would be difficult for human analysts to identify manually.

Machine learning systems are also widely used in healthcare, where they help analyze medical data and support diagnostic decisions. For example, machine learning models can examine medical images to detect signs of disease or analyze patient records to identify individuals at risk of certain conditions.

Despite its remarkable capabilities, machine learning is not without limitations. These systems depend heavily on the quality and diversity of the data used during training. If training datasets contain biases or incomplete information, the resulting models may produce biased predictions. Ensuring fairness and transparency in machine learning systems has therefore become an important area of research.

Another challenge involves the complexity of modern machine learning models. Some advanced systems operate as "black boxes," meaning their internal decision-making processes are difficult for humans to interpret. While these systems may produce highly accurate predictions, understanding how they arrive at those predictions can be challenging.

Nevertheless, the rise of machine learning systems represents one of the most significant technological shifts of the modern era. By enabling computers to learn from data rather than relying solely on fixed instructions, machine learning has opened new possibilities for automation, prediction, and intelligent decision-making.

As digital technologies continue to expand, machine learning will likely become even more integrated into everyday life. From personalized digital experiences to scientific research and industrial innovation, machine learning systems are reshaping how humans interact with technology and how complex problems are solved.

Understanding the rise of machine learning is essential for understanding the broader evolution of artificial intelligence. These systems form the foundation of many technologies that influence modern society, quietly analyzing patterns and making predictions that shape how information flows and how decisions are made in the digital world.

Predictive Analytics and Human Behavior Modeling

In the digital age, one of the most powerful capabilities of artificial intelligence and data science is the ability to anticipate human behavior before it happens. This capability is made possible through predictive analytics, a field that uses historical data, statistical algorithms, and machine learning techniques to forecast future outcomes. When applied to human activity, predictive analytics allow organizations to model behavior patterns and estimate how individuals or groups are likely to act in specific situations. This process, known as human behavior modeling, has become a central component of modern digital systems.

Predictive analytics operates on a simple but powerful principle: past behavior often provides clues about future behavior. Humans tend to follow patterns in how they make decisions, interact with information, and respond to incentives. By studying these patterns across large datasets, analysts and machine learning systems can identify trends that reveal underlying behavioral tendencies. Once these tendencies are understood, predictive models can estimate the probability of future actions with surprising accuracy.

The foundation of predictive analytics lies in data collection. Every digital interaction generates data points that describe how individuals behave. These interactions may include online searches, social media activity, video viewing habits, purchasing decisions, geographic movements, and many other forms of engagement. When millions or billions of such interactions are aggregated, they create datasets rich enough to reveal patterns in human behavior.

For example, when people shop online, their browsing activity reveals a great deal about their intentions. The products they view, the time they spend comparing items, and the sequence of pages they visit can signal whether they are simply exploring options or preparing to make a purchase. Predictive models analyze these behavioral signals and estimate the likelihood that a user will buy a particular product.

Similarly, digital platforms analyze patterns in content consumption to predict what users are most likely to watch, read, or listen to next. Streaming services examine viewing histories to anticipate which genres, actors, or storylines will appeal to specific audiences. Social media platforms monitor engagement patterns to determine which posts are most likely to capture attention and generate interaction.

Human behavior modeling extends beyond individual predictions to include patterns within groups and populations. By examining how large numbers of people behave in similar contexts, predictive systems can identify trends that influence entire communities. These models are particularly useful for businesses, governments, and researchers who seek to understand how behavior evolves over time.

The process of building predictive models typically involves several stages. The first stage is data preparation, where raw information is collected and organized into structured datasets. Because digital data often comes from multiple sources, it must be cleaned and standardized to ensure accuracy. This stage may involve removing incomplete records, correcting errors, and formatting data so it can be analyzed effectively.

The second stage involves feature extraction, where analysts identify variables that may influence behavior. Features might include demographic characteristics, browsing habits, purchase histories, or geographic locations. Each feature represents a potential factor that could help explain why individuals behave in certain ways.

Once relevant features are identified, machine learning algorithms are used to analyze relationships between variables. These algorithms examine patterns within the data and develop mathematical models that describe how different factors interact. For instance, a predictive model might discover that people who frequently search for travel destinations are more likely to purchase airline tickets within a certain timeframe.

After the model is trained on historical data, it can be applied to new situations. When fresh data becomes available, the model calculates probabilities for different outcomes. For example, an e-commerce platform might estimate the probability that a visitor will purchase a product, abandon their shopping cart, or leave the website without interacting further.

Predictive analytics is widely used across many industries. In marketing and advertising, predictive models help businesses identify potential customers and tailor marketing campaigns to their interests. By analyzing consumer behavior patterns, companies can determine which advertisements are most likely to influence purchasing decisions.

Retail companies often use predictive analytics to manage inventory and anticipate demand for products. By analyzing historical sales data and seasonal trends, retailers can estimate how many units of a product will be needed in the future. This allows them to optimize supply chains and reduce waste.

In the financial sector, predictive models are used to assess credit risk and detect fraudulent transactions. Banks analyze patterns in financial behavior to determine whether a loan applicant is likely to repay a debt. Similarly, fraud detection systems monitor transaction patterns and flag unusual activity that may indicate unauthorized access.

Healthcare has also benefited significantly from predictive analytics. Medical researchers analyze patient data to identify patterns associated with disease progression and treatment outcomes. Predictive models can help doctors estimate the risk of certain conditions, allowing for earlier intervention and personalized treatment plans.

Another important application of human behavior modeling is in urban planning and transportation systems. By analyzing traffic patterns, commuting habits, and population movement, city planners can design infrastructure that better accommodates the needs of residents. Predictive models help identify congestion points, optimize public transportation routes, and improve emergency response strategies.

In digital environments, predictive analytics plays a crucial role in shaping the user experience. Platforms use behavioral models to personalize content feeds, recommend products, and deliver targeted advertisements. The goal is to present information that users are most likely to find interesting or useful, thereby increasing engagement and satisfaction.

However, the growing use of predictive analytics also raises important ethical and societal questions. One concern involves privacy. Because predictive models rely on large amounts of personal data, users may feel uncomfortable with the extent to which their behavior is monitored and analyzed. Even when data is anonymized, detailed behavioral patterns can sometimes reveal sensitive information about individuals.

Another concern relates to the potential for algorithmic bias. If the datasets used to train predictive models contain biases or inaccuracies, the resulting predictions may reinforce those biases. For example, if historical data reflects unequal treatment of certain groups, predictive systems may unintentionally replicate those disparities in their recommendations or decisions.

Transparency is therefore an important aspect of responsible predictive analytics. Organizations that use behavioral models must ensure that their systems are designed with fairness and accountability in mind. Clear explanations of how predictions are generated can help build trust among users and stakeholders.

Despite these challenges, predictive analytics remains one of the most powerful tools available for understanding human behavior. By analyzing vast datasets and identifying patterns within them, predictive models can reveal insights that were previously impossible to detect. These insights help organizations make informed decisions, anticipate future trends, and respond more effectively to changing conditions.

Human behavior modeling demonstrates how closely technology and psychology have become intertwined in the digital age. Every interaction with digital systems contributes to a growing body of knowledge about how people think, choose, and act. When this information is processed through advanced analytical techniques, it enables machines to forecast behavior with remarkable precision.

As predictive technologies continue to evolve, their influence will likely expand across many aspects of daily life. From personalized recommendations to large-scale social analysis, predictive analytics will remain a central force shaping how information flows and how decisions are made in the modern world.

How AI Understands Personality, Emotions, and Intent

Artificial intelligence has evolved far beyond simple data processing. Modern AI systems are increasingly capable of interpreting complex aspects of human behavior, including personality traits, emotional states, and underlying intentions. By analyzing large volumes of behavioral data, language patterns, and digital interactions, AI can develop surprisingly detailed insights into how individuals think and feel. These capabilities have transformed fields such as marketing, social media, customer service, and behavioral research, making AI an important tool for understanding human psychology in the digital age.

The ability of AI to interpret personality, emotions, and intent relies primarily on data analysis and pattern recognition. Human behavior leaves digital traces in many forms, including written text, spoken language, facial expressions, browsing patterns, and social media interactions. When these signals are collected across millions of users, machine learning systems can identify correlations between observable behaviors and psychological characteristics.

One of the most widely studied methods for analyzing personality through digital data involves behavioral profiling. Behavioral profiling examines patterns in how individuals interact with digital platforms. The types of content people engage with, the frequency of their interactions, and the subjects they discuss online can all provide clues about their personality traits.

For example, someone who frequently engages with social discussions, shares opinions publicly, and interacts with a large network of contacts may display traits associated with extroversion. In contrast, individuals who interact less frequently or focus on niche topics may exhibit characteristics associated with introversion. While these patterns do not define personality completely, they provide signals that machine learning systems can analyze and interpret.

Psychological models such as the Big Five personality framework are often used in AI-based personality analysis. The Big Five model describes personality along five dimensions: openness, conscientiousness, extraversion, agreeableness, and neuroticism. Researchers have found that language use, social behavior, and digital activity often correlate with these personality traits. By examining word choices, communication patterns, and interaction styles, AI systems can estimate where individuals may fall within these categories.

Language analysis plays a crucial role in understanding both personality and emotion. Advances in natural language processing (NLP) allow AI systems to analyze text and identify subtle patterns in how people communicate. Words, sentence structures, and writing styles often reveal emotional states or underlying attitudes.

For instance, language filled with enthusiastic expressions and positive adjectives may indicate excitement or happiness, while messages containing negative language or frustration-related words may suggest dissatisfaction or stress. AI models trained on large datasets of human communication can detect these patterns and classify emotional tone with considerable accuracy.

Social media platforms provide rich datasets for this type of analysis. Users frequently express their thoughts, opinions, and feelings through posts, comments, and messages. By analyzing these expressions across large populations, machine learning systems learn how specific linguistic patterns correspond to emotional states.

In addition to text, AI can analyze visual signals to detect emotions. Computer vision technologies allow systems to interpret facial expressions, body language, and gestures. Cameras and image recognition algorithms can identify subtle changes in facial muscles that correspond to emotions such as happiness, sadness, surprise, or anger.

For example, when a person smiles, specific facial muscles contract in recognizable patterns. AI models trained on thousands of images can detect these patterns and infer emotional states. Similarly, raised eyebrows, narrowed eyes, or downward facial movements may signal different emotional responses.

Voice analysis is another important tool used by AI to interpret emotions and intent. Speech contains not only words but also variations in tone, pitch, speed, and rhythm. Changes in these vocal characteristics can reveal emotional states such as excitement, anxiety, or frustration. AI-powered speech recognition systems analyze these acoustic features to determine how someone feels while speaking.

Intent detection represents another key capability of modern AI systems. Understanding intent involves identifying the purpose behind a user's actions or communication. For example, when someone searches online for "best laptops for graphic design," the intent behind the query is not merely informational. The user may be planning to purchase a device and is researching options.

AI systems analyze context and behavioral patterns to interpret these intentions. Search queries, browsing history, and click behavior provide clues about what users hope to accomplish. By understanding intent, platforms can deliver more relevant responses, recommendations, or advertisements.

Customer service applications often rely heavily on intent recognition. When users communicate with chatbots or virtual assistants, AI systems analyze the language used in messages to determine the user's request. The system may classify the intent as seeking technical support, requesting product information, or attempting to resolve a billing issue. Once the intent is identified, the system can provide an appropriate response.

The ability to interpret emotions and intent has significant implications for digital personalization. Platforms that understand user psychology can tailor experiences that feel more responsive and engaging. Streaming services recommend content aligned with emotional preferences, online stores suggest products that match lifestyle choices, and social media platforms prioritize posts likely to generate emotional engagement.

In marketing, AI-driven emotional and personality analysis allows advertisers to design messages that resonate more deeply with specific audiences. By identifying which emotional triggers are most effective for different groups, companies can craft campaigns that align with consumer motivations. For example, advertisements emphasizing excitement and novelty may appeal to individuals who exhibit high openness, while messages focusing on reliability and security may attract those with higher conscientiousness.

Despite these advantages, the ability of AI to analyze personality and emotions also raises important ethical questions. One concern involves privacy. Many users are unaware of how much information about their psychological tendencies can be inferred from digital behavior. Data collected from social media interactions, browsing habits, and communication patterns can reveal insights that individuals may consider highly personal.

Another concern involves the potential for behavioral manipulation. If AI systems can accurately detect emotional states or personality traits, they may also be able to exploit those insights to influence decisions. For instance, marketing campaigns might target individuals during moments when they are more emotionally vulnerable or more receptive to persuasion.

Researchers and policymakers have therefore emphasized the importance of responsible AI development. Ethical guidelines encourage transparency about how behavioral data is used and promote safeguards to prevent misuse of psychological insights. Regulations in some regions require companies to obtain consent before collecting certain types of personal data.

Despite these challenges, the ability of artificial intelligence to understand personality, emotions, and intent continues to expand. Advances in machine learning, natural language processing, and computer vision are making it possible to interpret human signals with increasing accuracy. These technologies are being applied not only in commercial settings but also in healthcare, education, and mental health support systems.

For example, AI-driven emotional analysis tools are being developed to assist therapists in monitoring patient well-being or to detect early signs of depression through speech and text analysis. In education, AI systems may analyze student engagement and emotional responses to improve learning experiences.

Understanding how AI interprets personality and emotion is essential for understanding the broader relationship between humans and intelligent machines. Digital technologies are no longer passive tools that simply execute commands. Instead, they actively analyze human behavior, learn from it, and respond in ways that influence future interactions.

As these systems become more sophisticated, they will continue to shape how individuals communicate, make decisions, and interact with digital environments. Recognizing the mechanisms behind AI-driven psychological analysis allows individuals to better understand the invisible processes guiding many aspects of modern technology.

In the digital age, the boundary between technology and human psychology is becoming increasingly intertwined. Artificial intelligence systems that interpret personality, emotions, and intent represent one of the most powerful examples of this convergence. By transforming behavioral data into psychological insights, AI is redefining how machines understand and interact with the human mind.

When Machines Begin to Influence Human Decisions

For most of human history, decisions were shaped primarily by human judgment, personal experience, and social influence. Individuals relied on their own reasoning, advice from others, and available information to determine what actions to take. However, the rise of digital technologies and artificial intelligence has introduced a new factor into the decision-making process: machines that actively guide and influence human choices. As algorithms and AI systems become more sophisticated, they increasingly participate in the process by which people evaluate options, form opinions, and make decisions.

This influence does not usually occur through direct commands or obvious instructions. Instead, machines shape decisions subtly by organizing information, recommending options, and prioritizing certain choices over others. Because humans depend heavily on digital platforms for information and communication, the systems that control those platforms play a powerful role in determining what people see and how they interpret the world around them.

One of the most common ways machines influence decisions is through recommendation systems. These systems analyze user behavior and suggest products, content, or services that match a person's interests. When users open a streaming platform, an online store, or a social media application, they often encounter recommendations generated by algorithms. These suggestions guide users toward specific choices, shaping what they watch, buy, or read.

For example, when a video platform recommends a particular documentary or series, many viewers choose to watch it simply because it appears prominently on their screen. In this situation, the algorithm does not force the decision but frames the available options in a way that increases the likelihood of a certain outcome. By presenting some choices more visibly than others, the machine influences which decisions feel most convenient or appealing.

Online shopping platforms operate in a similar way. Algorithms analyze past purchases and browsing patterns to recommend products that users may want to buy. Sections such as "Recommended for You" or "Customers Also Bought" encourage individuals to consider items they might not have searched for independently. Over time, these recommendations shape purchasing habits and guide consumers toward brands or categories.

Artificial intelligence also influences decisions through search engine rankings. When people search for information online, they typically focus on the first few results displayed on the search page. Because search engines rank these results using algorithms, the ranking system plays a significant role in shaping what information users encounter first.

Studies have shown that individuals are far more likely to click on links that appear near the top of search results than those listed further down the page. As a result, the algorithm that determines search rankings indirectly influences what information people trust and how they form opinions about various topics. In many cases, users assume that highly ranked results are more reliable or authoritative simply because they appear first.

Another area where machines influence decisions is navigation and transportation. Many people rely on digital navigation systems to determine the fastest routes when traveling. These systems analyze traffic conditions, road closures, and travel patterns to recommend routes that minimize travel time. While this guidance is often helpful, it also means that drivers frequently follow the directions suggested by the algorithm rather than relying on their own judgment.

In some cases, navigation algorithms can alter traffic patterns within entire cities. If a navigation system directs large numbers of drivers along a particular route, congestion may shift from major roads to smaller streets. This illustrates how algorithmic guidance can influence not only individual decisions but also broader social dynamics.

Artificial intelligence is also widely used in financial decision making. Banks and financial institutions rely on predictive models to assess creditworthiness and evaluate loan applications. These models analyze historical data, including income levels, credit history, and spending behavior, to estimate the likelihood that a borrower will repay a loan.

While these systems can process information more efficiently than human analysts, they also influence who receives financial opportunities and who does not. The decisions generated by algorithms can affect access to credit, housing, and investment opportunities. As a result, machine-driven assessments increasingly shape the economic decisions that influence people's lives.

In the workplace, algorithms are often used to assist with hiring decisions. Some companies use AI-powered systems to analyze job applications, screen resumes, and identify candidates who match certain qualifications. These systems evaluate factors such as experience, skills, and past employment patterns to recommend applicants for interviews.

Although these tools can help employers process large numbers of applications, they also introduce new complexities into the hiring process. Because the algorithms determine which candidates receive attention, they indirectly influence career opportunities and professional advancement.

Healthcare represents another domain where machine influence is growing. Artificial intelligence systems can analyze medical records, diagnostic images, and genetic data to assist doctors in making treatment decisions. In some cases, AI systems may detect patterns in medical data that human physicians might overlook.

When doctors rely on these systems for guidance, the algorithm's analysis becomes part of the decision-making process. While this collaboration between humans and machines can improve medical outcomes, it also raises questions about how much authority should be given to automated recommendations.

The influence of machines on human decisions is particularly strong in digital media environments. Social media algorithms determine which posts appear in users' feeds based on engagement signals such as likes, shares, and comments. Because users typically see only a fraction of the available content, the algorithm plays a critical role in shaping the information they encounter.

Content that generates strong reactions—whether positive or negative—is often promoted more widely because it attracts higher engagement. As a result, the algorithm may amplify certain narratives, ideas, or emotional responses, influencing how individuals perceive events and issues.

This influence becomes especially significant when people rely on digital platforms as primary sources of news and information. The stories that algorithms highlight can shape public discourse, determine which topics receive attention, and influence how individuals interpret social and political events.

Another factor that increases the influence of machines is the psychological tendency to trust automated systems. Humans often assume that algorithmic decisions are objective or data driven. Because machines are perceived as analytical and impartial, people may accept algorithmic recommendations with less skepticism than they would apply to advice from other humans.

This phenomenon, sometimes referred to as automation bias, can lead individuals to rely heavily on machine-generated suggestions even when those suggestions may not be entirely accurate. In situations where algorithms provide guidance quickly and confidently, users may follow the recommendation without thoroughly evaluating alternative options.

Despite the growing influence of machines, it is important to recognize that humans still retain the ability to make independent choices. Algorithms may shape the options presented, but individuals ultimately decide whether to accept or reject those suggestions. Awareness of how algorithmic systems operate can help people maintain greater control over their decisions.

Transparency in algorithm design is also becoming an important topic in discussions about artificial intelligence. Researchers and policymakers are exploring ways to ensure that users understand how recommendations are generated and how automated systems influence choices. Providing explanations for algorithmic decisions may help individuals evaluate suggestions more critically.

As artificial intelligence continues to evolve, the interaction between humans and machines will likely become even more complex. Decision-making processes in areas such as finance, healthcare, transportation, and communication will increasingly involve collaboration between human judgment and machine intelligence.

The moment when machines begin to influence human decisions marks a significant turning point in technological history. Algorithms no longer simply process information; they actively participate in shaping the choices people make. By organizing options, predicting preferences, and recommending actions, machines have become powerful participants in the decision-making landscape of the modern world.

Understanding this influence is essential for navigating the digital age responsibly. Recognizing how machines shape decisions allow individuals to remain aware of the forces guiding their choices. In a world where algorithms are deeply integrated into everyday life, the ability to think critically about machine-generated recommendations may become one of the most important skills for preserving human autonomy.

Chapter 5

social media and the Engineering of Engagement

Social media has become one of the most influential technological forces of the twenty-first century. Platforms designed to connect people across the world have transformed how individuals communicate, share information, and interact with society. What began as simple digital spaces for maintaining friendships and exchanging messages has evolved into complex ecosystems powered by algorithms, data analytics, and artificial intelligence. These systems are not merely tools for communication; they are sophisticated environments engineered to capture and sustain human attention.

At the center of this transformation lies the concept of engagement. In the context of social media, engagement refers to the actions users take when interacting with content. These actions include liking posts, sharing information, commenting on discussions, watching videos, following accounts, and spending time browsing through feeds. Every interaction provides a measurable signal indicating that the content has successfully captured the user's attention.

For social media companies, engagement is far more than a measure of user activity. It is the foundation of their business models. Most major platforms generate revenue through advertising, and advertising revenue depends heavily on the amount of time users spend interacting with the platform. The longer individuals remain active on a service, the more opportunities exist to display advertisements and collect behavioral data. As a result, social media platforms have strong incentives to design systems that maximize user engagement.

To achieve this goal, companies rely on a combination of behavioral psychology, data science, and algorithmic design. Social media platforms continuously analyze user behavior to understand what types of content attract attention and generate reactions. Every scroll, click, or comment becomes part of a dataset that helps algorithms learn how to keep users engaged.

These algorithms play a central role in determining what users see when they open their social media applications. Because the amount of content produced every day is far greater than any individual could realistically view, platforms must decide which posts to display and in what order. Rather than presenting content chronologically, many social media systems rely on algorithmic ranking models that prioritize posts most likely to generate interaction.

The ranking process typically considers multiple factors, including how frequently a user interacts with a particular account, how many people are responding to a specific post, and how long users tend to spend viewing similar types of content. By analyzing these signals, algorithms attempt to predict which posts will capture a user's attention most effectively.

This process represents a shift from simple information sharing to what many researchers describe as the engineering of engagement. Instead of passively hosting user-generated content, social media platforms actively shape the digital environment in order to maximize interaction. The design of notifications, the arrangement of feeds, and the structure of content recommendations are all carefully calibrated to encourage continuous participation.

Psychological principles play an important role in this design strategy. Humans are naturally drawn to novelty, social validation, and emotionally stimulating content. Social media platforms leverage these tendencies by highlighting posts that generate strong reactions and by providing immediate feedback through likes, comments, and notifications. Each notification acts as a signal that someone has responded to a user's activity, creating a cycle of anticipation and reward.

The use of infinite scrolling interfaces is another example of engagement engineering. Instead of presenting content in fixed pages, many platforms allow users to scroll endlessly through their feeds. As new content continuously appears, users are encouraged to keep browsing in search of the next interesting post. This design removes natural stopping points that might otherwise prompt users to disengage.

Another feature that contributes to sustained engagement is the use of algorithmic recommendations. Social media platforms analyze user behavior to identify topics, creators, or communities that align with personal interests. By recommending relevant content, platforms ensure that users frequently encounter posts that resonate with their preferences.

These systems are not static. Algorithms constantly adjust in response to changing patterns of user behavior. If a particular type of content begins attracting more attention, the system may increase its visibility across the platform. In this way, social media environments evolve dynamically based on collective engagement patterns.

While the engineering of engagement has enabled social media platforms to grow rapidly, it has also sparked widespread debate about the broader consequences of these systems. Critics argue that algorithms designed to maximize engagement may unintentionally amplify sensational or emotionally charged content because such material often generates strong reactions. Others have raised concerns about how algorithmic curation influences public discourse and shapes perceptions of social and political issues.

Supporters, however, emphasize the positive aspects of engagement-driven platforms. Social media has allowed individuals to share ideas, build communities, and access information in ways that were not possible in earlier eras. Many users rely on these platforms for education, professional networking, and social support.

Understanding how engagement is engineered within social media systems is essential for understanding the broader relationship between technology and human attention. The design of these platforms reflects a powerful intersection between psychology, economics, and artificial intelligence. Every feature, from recommendation algorithms to notification systems, contributes to a carefully constructed environment that encourages continuous interaction.

As social media continues to evolve, the dynamics of engagement will likely become even more sophisticated. Advances in machine learning and behavioral analytics will enable platforms to predict user responses with greater precision and adapt their systems accordingly. The result will be digital environments that are increasingly personalized and responsive to individual behavior.

This chapter explores how social media platforms are designed to capture and maintain attention. By examining the technological and psychological mechanisms behind engagement engineering, it becomes possible to understand how these systems influence user behavior and shape the flow of information in the digital age.

The Design of Infinite Scroll and Endless Feeds

One of the most influential design innovations in modern digital platforms is the concept of infinite scroll and endless content feeds. At first glance, this design appears simple: users scroll down a screen, and new content continuously appears without interruption. However, behind this seemingly straightforward feature lies a carefully engineered system designed to maximize user engagement and maintain attention for as long as possible. Infinite scroll has become a central element of social media platforms, news websites, and content-sharing services, fundamentally shaping how people consume digital information.

Before the introduction of infinite scrolling interfaces, most websites relied on pagination, a structure that divided content into separate pages. Users would read the material on one page and then click a button to navigate to the next page. This structure created natural stopping points. When a page ended, users often paused, reflected on what they had seen, and decided whether they wanted to continue browsing or move on to another activity.

Infinite scroll removed these natural pauses. Instead of presenting information in discrete pages, the interface loads additional content automatically as the user reaches the bottom of the screen. The result is a continuous stream of information that can theoretically extend without limit. Users do not need to take deliberate action to load more content; the system delivers it seamlessly.

From a design perspective, infinite scroll reduces friction. Friction refers to any barrier that slows down or interrupts user interaction. By eliminating the need to click “next page” or navigate between sections, infinite scrolling allows users to remain immersed in the browsing experience. The absence of interruption makes it easier for individuals to continue scrolling without consciously deciding to do so.

The effectiveness of infinite scrolls is closely connected to human psychology. Humans have a natural curiosity about what comes next, a trait sometimes described as the “information gap.” When individuals encounter a stream of content, they often feel compelled to continue exploring to discover the next interesting item. Infinite scrolling exploits this curiosity by constantly presenting new material just beyond the current screen.

Another psychological factor that contributes to the effectiveness of endless feeds is the principle of variable reward. Variable reward systems deliver outcomes unpredictably rather than on a fixed schedule. This unpredictability keeps users engaged because they never know when the next piece of content will be particularly interesting, entertaining, or emotionally stimulating.

In the context of social media, each post encountered while scrolling represents a potential reward. Some posts may be ordinary or uninteresting, while others may be humorous, surprising, or personally meaningful. Because users cannot predict when the next rewarding piece of content will appear, they often continue scrolling in anticipation of finding something engaging.

This reward pattern resembles mechanisms used in other forms of entertainment, such as video games and gambling systems, where intermittent rewards encourage repeated participation. In digital platforms, the endless feed becomes a mechanism that encourages prolonged interaction through the promise of discovering the next appealing post.

The design of infinite scroll also benefits from algorithmic personalization. Modern platforms rarely present random content in endless feeds. Instead, algorithms analyze user behavior and select posts that align with individual interests. As users interact with content by liking, sharing, or watching videos, the system collects data that helps refine future recommendations.

This personalization increases the probability that users will encounter content that resonates with them. When the feed consistently displays topics, creators, or ideas that match a user's preferences, the scrolling experience becomes more engaging. Each new item appears relevant, reinforcing the desire to continue browsing.

Another important design element in endless feeds is the rapid presentation of content. Posts are typically arranged in short, easily digestible formats that require minimal effort to consume. Images, brief videos, short text updates, and headlines allow users to process information quickly and move on to the next item.

This rapid consumption style encourages continuous scrolling because each piece of content demands only a small amount of attention. Unlike long articles or detailed reports that require sustained focus, feed-based content can be evaluated within seconds. If a post fails to capture interest immediately, users can simply scroll past it.

Notifications and interaction feature further enhance the effectiveness of endless feeds. When users receive alerts about new comments, likes, or messages, they are encouraged to return to the platform. Once they reopen the application, they often reenter the scrolling cycle, exploring new content in their feed.

Social elements also play a role in maintaining engagement. Seeing posts from friends, influencers, or communities creates a sense of connection and relevance. Users may feel motivated to stay updated on what others are sharing or discussing. This social context reinforces the value of continuing to scroll.

The economic incentives behind infinite scrolling are closely tied to the attention economy. Digital platforms generate revenue primarily through advertising. Advertisements are displayed within the content feed, often appearing between posts or videos. The longer users remain active on the platform, the more advertisements they encounter.

By encouraging extended browsing sessions, infinite scroll increases the total amount of time users spend on the platform. This extended engagement creates additional opportunities for advertisements to be viewed and for user behavior to be analyzed. As a result, the design of endless feeds directly supports the financial models of many digital services.

Despite its effectiveness in sustaining engagement, infinite scrolling has also raised concerns about its impact on user well-being and attention patterns. Because the design removes natural stopping points, individuals may lose track of time while browsing. What begins as a brief visit to check updates can easily turn into extended periods of continuous scrolling.

Researchers have observed that prolonged exposure to endless feeds can contribute to digital fatigue, reduced concentration, and difficulty disengaging from online content. The constant availability of new information can make it challenging for users to recognize when they have consumed enough content for a given session.

Another concern involves the potential for information overload. Endless feeds present large volumes of content within short time frames. While this abundance can be entertaining, it may also make it difficult for users to process information deeply or reflect on what they have encountered. Important ideas may appear briefly in the field and then disappear as new content replaces them.

Some technology companies have begun exploring ways to balance engagement with user well-being. Features such as screen-time reminders, activity dashboards, and content limits aim to help users become more aware of their browsing habits. These tools encourage individuals to monitor how much time they spend interacting with digital platforms.

Design researchers have also discussed alternative interface structures that introduce intentional pauses or encourage more thoughtful content consumption. While infinite scrolling remains dominant across many platforms, discussions about healthier digital design continue to grow.

Despite these concerns, infinite scroll remains one of the most powerful engagement mechanisms in modern technology. Its success demonstrates how subtle design choices can significantly influence user behavior. By combining psychological principles, algorithmic recommendations, and frictionless interfaces, endless feeds create digital environments that encourage continuous exploration.

Understanding the design of infinite scrolling helps reveal how digital platforms shape the flow of attention in the online world. What appears to be a simple interface feature is part of a larger system designed to capture curiosity, deliver rewards, and sustain engagement over extended periods.

As technology evolves and digital experiences become more immersive, the principles behind infinite scrolling will likely continue influencing how information is presented and consumed. Recognizing how these systems operate allows users to approach digital environments with greater awareness, understanding the subtle design strategies that encourage them to keep scrolling long after they first open their screens.

Notifications, Alerts, and Psychological Triggers

In the modern digital environment, notifications and alerts have become an integral part of how people interact with technology. Every day, smartphones, computers, and wearable devices deliver countless notification messages, reminders, updates, and alerts that demand attention. While these signals often serve practical purposes, such as informing users about new messages or upcoming events, they are also carefully designed mechanisms that shape how individuals engage with digital platforms. Behind each notification lies a combination of behavioral psychology, data analytics, and user experience design intended to capture attention and encourage continued interaction.

At their core, notifications are tools for re-engagement. Digital platforms compete intensely for user attention, and notifications provide a direct channel through which applications can draw users back into their environments. When a device vibrates, flashes a message, or produces a sound, it interrupts the user's current activity and signals that something requires attention. This interruption can create a sense of urgency, prompting individuals to check their devices even when they had not intended to do so.

The effectiveness of notifications is deeply rooted in human psychological responses to stimuli. Humans are naturally sensitive to sudden signals, such as sounds, vibrations, or visual changes. These signals historically served as survival mechanisms, alerting individuals to potential threats or important environmental changes. In the digital context, notification sounds and visual badges activate similar responses, triggering immediate curiosity about the source of the alert.

One of the most powerful psychological principles used in notification systems is intermittent reinforcement. Intermittent reinforcement refers to reward systems where outcomes occur unpredictably rather than on a fixed schedule. Behavioral psychologists have long observed that unpredictable rewards tend to produce stronger and more persistent engagement than predictable ones.

Notifications operate within this framework by delivering alerts that may or may not correspond to something meaningful or rewarding. Sometimes a notification signals an exciting message from a friend, a positive comment on a post, or an interesting piece of content. Other times, it may simply be a reminder or an automated update. Because users cannot predict which notifications will be rewarding, they often check every alert in anticipation of discovering something valuable.

This anticipation creates a habit loop consisting of three main stages: cue, action, and reward. The notification acts as the cue that captures attention. The user responds by opening the application or checking the device. If the user encounters rewarding experiences such as social approval, entertainment, or useful information—the brain associates the behavior with a positive outcome. Over time, this cycle reinforces the habit of responding to notifications quickly and frequently.

Social media platforms have refined this habit loop with remarkable precision. Notifications often inform users when someone has liked their post, commented on their content, or mentioned them in a discussion. These alerts tap into a fundamental human desire for social validation. Positive feedback from others provides emotional rewards that reinforce continued participation in the platform.

The design of notification systems often emphasizes visual cues that attract attention. Small icons, colored badges, and numerical indicators signal that new activity has occurred. The use of bright colors, particularly red or orange, is intentional because these colors naturally draw the human eye and convey urgency. A small red badge displaying a number of unread messages can create a psychological impulse to clear the notification by opening the application.

Sound and vibration patterns also contribute to the effectiveness of notifications. Distinctive tones or haptic feedback signals allow users to recognize alerts even without looking at their screens. These signals create a direct connection between the platform and the user's sensory perception, ensuring that notifications are noticed quickly.

Another factor that increases the influence of notifications is timing. Modern digital platforms often use machine learning algorithms to determine when users are most likely to respond to alerts. By analyzing behavioral patterns—such as when individuals typically check their devices or interact with application systems can deliver notifications at moments when engagement is most probable.

For example, if a platform detects that a user frequently checks their phone during commuting hours or late in the evening, it may schedule notifications during those periods. This targeted timing increases the likelihood that the user will open the application and interact with the content.

Notifications are also used strategically to encourage users to return after periods of inactivity. If someone has not opened an application for several days, the system may send reminders about new content, updates from friends, or trending topics. These reminders serve as prompts designed to reactivate engagement and reintroduce users to the platform's environment.

The influence of notifications extends beyond simple engagement. They can also shape decision-making and behavior patterns. For instance, e-commerce platforms may send alerts about limited-time discounts or product availability. These notifications often create a sense of urgency, encouraging users to act quickly before an opportunity appears to disappear.

Similarly, news applications may send breaking news alerts that prompt users to open articles immediately. Because these alerts are framed as urgent or important, they can influence which stories receive the most attention and how individuals stay informed about current events.

While notifications offer many practical benefits, their widespread use has also raised concerns about their impact on attention and mental well-being. Frequent interruptions can fragment concentration and make it difficult to focus on tasks that require sustained attention. Studies have shown that even brief interruptions can disrupt cognitive processes, reduce productivity and increasing mental fatigue.

Another issue involves the potential for notification overload. As individuals install more applications on their devices, the number of alerts they receive may increase dramatically. Multiple notifications arriving throughout the day can create a constant sense of distraction, making it difficult to disconnect from digital environments.

Some users respond to this challenge by adjusting notification settings or disabling alerts for certain applications. Technology companies have also introduced tools that allow individuals to manage their notification preferences more effectively. Features such as notification summaries, focus modes, and customizable alerts help users control when and how they receive digital interruptions.

Despite these efforts, notifications remain one of the most powerful engagement mechanisms in modern technology. Their effectiveness lies in their ability to combine psychological triggers with data-driven personalization. By understanding when users are most receptive and what types of alerts generate the strongest responses, platforms can design notification systems that encourage consistent interaction.

From a broader perspective, notifications illustrate how digital systems are designed to compete for human attention. In an environment where countless applications and services seek engagement, the ability to deliver timely and compelling alerts becomes a critical advantage.

Understanding the psychology behind notifications allows individuals to become more aware of how these systems influence their behavior. Recognizing the cues, rewards, and habit loops embedded within notification design can help users make more deliberate choices about when and how they engage with digital platforms.

As technology continues to evolve, the role of notifications will likely expand further. Advances in artificial intelligence and behavioral analytics may enable systems to deliver even more personalized alerts tailored to individual preferences and routines. While these developments may improve convenience and connectivity, they will also deepen the relationship between digital systems and human attention.

In the end, notifications are far more than simple reminders or updates. They are carefully engineered signals designed to capture curiosity, trigger habits, and guide behavior within the digital ecosystem. By understanding how these mechanisms operate, individuals can navigate digital environments with greater awareness and maintain a healthier balance between technology and attention.

Viral Content and Emotional Amplification

In the digital age, information can spread across the world at extraordinary speed. A single post, video, or image can reach millions of people within hours, traveling across social media platforms, messaging networks, and online communities. This phenomenon is commonly referred to as viral content. While viral content may appear spontaneous or unpredictable, its spread is often closely connected to emotional responses and the design of modern digital platforms. Emotions play a central role in determining what people share, discuss, and react to online, and algorithms frequently amplify content that generates strong emotional engagement.

The concept of virality is closely related to the structure of networked communication systems. Social media platforms allow individuals to distribute information instantly to large audiences. When users share a piece of content, it becomes visible to their followers or contacts. If those viewers decide to share it further, the content travels across additional networks. This chain reaction allows information to spread exponentially as each new participant extends the reach of the original post.

However, not all content spreads at the same rate. Most posts receive little attention, while a small percentage achieve massive visibility. The key difference often lies in the emotional impact of the content. Research into online behavior consistently shows that content provoking strong emotional reactions is significantly more likely to be shared than neutral information.

Emotions such as excitement, amusement, anger, surprise, and fear tend to stimulate higher levels of engagement. When individuals encounter material that triggers these feelings, they may feel compelled to express their reactions by liking, commenting, or sharing the content with others. These actions generate signals that algorithms interpret as indicators of relevance or importance.

Once a post begins receiving significant engagement, algorithms may increase its visibility across the platform. Social media systems are designed to highlight content that attracts attention because such content keeps users active and interacting with the platform. As engagement increases, the algorithm may promote the post to additional audiences, further accelerating its spread.

This process creates a feedback cycle in which emotionally engaging content receives algorithmic amplification. The more reactions a post generates, the more prominently it is displayed. Increased visibility leads to additional reactions, which in turn lead to even greater distribution. Over time, this cycle can transform a simple post into viral content reaching millions of viewers.

Positive emotions often play an important role in viral content. Humorous videos, inspiring stories, and entertaining challenges frequently achieve widespread popularity because they evoke feelings of joy or amusement. People enjoy sharing content that makes others laugh or feel inspired, and these emotional experiences encourage further distribution.

However, negative emotions can also drive virality, sometimes even more powerful than positive ones. Content that triggers outrage, fear, or moral indignation often spreads rapidly because individuals feel motivated to express their reactions or alert others. Posts highlighting controversial topics, perceived injustices, or alarming events frequently attract intense engagement.

One reason negative emotions can amplify viral spread is that they activate social identity and group dynamics. When individuals encounter content that challenges their beliefs or values, they may share it in order to defend their perspectives or mobilize support from others who share similar views. This process can lead to highly active discussions and rapid circulation of emotionally charged material.

Digital platforms amplify these emotional responses through engagement-based ranking systems. Algorithms often measure the success of content using metrics such as likes, comments, shares, and viewing time. Because emotionally stimulating posts tend to generate more interactions, they naturally rise within the ranking system and become more visible to users.

Video content provides a particularly strong example of emotional amplification. Videos can combine visual imagery, music, storytelling, and editing techniques to evoke powerful emotional responses. Platforms that host video content often prioritize clips that capture viewers' attention for longer periods. If a video generates high watch times and strong reactions, algorithms may recommend it to broader audiences.

Short-form video platforms have demonstrated how quickly viral content can spread when emotional engagement and algorithmic recommendation systems work together. A video that resonates with viewers may appear repeatedly in recommendation feeds, allowing it to reach users who have never encountered the creator before. Each new viewer becomes a potential participant in the sharing process.

Memes represent another form of viral content driven by emotional amplification. Memes often combine humor, cultural references, and simple visual elements to communicate ideas quickly. Because they are easy to understand and replicate, memes spread rapidly across digital communities. Their emotional appeal encourages users to share them with friends and adapt them into new variations.

The speed of viral spread is also influenced by platform design features that facilitate sharing. Social media applications typically include simple buttons for reposting or forwarding content. With a single tap, users can distribute material to their networks without significant effort. This ease of sharing removes barriers that might otherwise slow the spread of information.

While viral content can entertain and inspire, it also presents challenges for the digital information ecosystem. One concern is that emotionally amplified content may spread regardless of its accuracy or reliability. Sensational stories, misleading headlines, or manipulated media can attract strong reactions even if the information they contain is incomplete or incorrect.

When algorithms prioritize engagement rather than accuracy, emotionally charged misinformation may gain visibility before fact-checking processes can intervene. This dynamic has raised concerns among researchers and policymakers about the potential for viral content to influence public opinion or spread misleading narratives.

Another issue related to emotional amplification is polarization. Content that evokes strong emotional reactions may reinforce existing divisions between groups with different viewpoints. When individuals encounter material that confirms their beliefs or criticizes opposing perspectives, they may engage more actively with that content. This engagement encourages algorithms to deliver similar material in the future, strengthening the cycle.

Despite these challenges, viral content also offers positive opportunities for communication and social change. Important messages about public health, humanitarian efforts, or social awareness campaigns can reach large audiences when they resonate emotionally with viewers. Viral movements and online campaigns have mobilized support for charitable causes, environmental initiatives, and social justice efforts.

Creators and organizations often attempt to design content with viral potential by incorporating emotional storytelling, compelling visuals, and relatable themes. While it is impossible to guarantee that a post will become viral, understanding the emotional triggers that drive sharing can increase the likelihood that content will capture attention.

From a broader perspective, the relationship between emotion and virality reflects fundamental aspects of human communication. Throughout history, stories that evoke strong feelings have been more memorable and more likely to be passed from one person to another. Digital platforms have accelerated this process by enabling rapid global distribution.

As social media continues to evolve, the mechanisms behind viral content will likely become even more sophisticated. Advances in artificial intelligence and behavioral analytics allow platforms to predict which types of content are most likely to generate emotional engagement. These insights enable algorithms to refine recommendation systems and deliver posts that maximize interaction.

Understanding viral content and emotional amplification is essential for navigating the modern information landscape. Recognizing how emotions influence sharing behavior can help individuals approach online material with greater awareness and critical thinking. By understanding the forces that drive virality, users can better evaluate the content they encounter and make informed decisions about what they choose to share.

In the digital age, viral content is not merely a random phenomenon but a reflection of how human emotions interact with technological systems. Algorithms amplify the signals created by emotional responses, transforming individual reactions into large-scale patterns of information distribution. As a result, the emotional dynamics of human behavior continue to shape the flow of ideas, stories, and conversations across the global digital network.

Conclusion

The modern digital world has introduced a profound transformation in how information is created, distributed, and consumed. What once required newspapers, television broadcasts, and physical communication networks can now occur instantly through interconnected digital platforms. Within this environment, artificial intelligence, algorithms, and data-driven systems play a central role in shaping how people interact with information and with one another. The journey explored throughout this book reveals how the digital ecosystem has evolved into a powerful system capable of influencing attention, behavior, and decision-making on a global scale.

At the heart of this transformation lies the concept of human attention. Attention has become one of the most valuable resources in the digital economy. Platforms compete intensely to capture and retain it because attention drives engagement, and engagement fuels the economic engines behind advertising, data collection, and digital services. Every scroll, click, and interaction contributes to a vast network of signals that algorithms use to refine their understanding of human behavior.

Artificial intelligence systems have become increasingly effective at analyzing these signals. Through machine learning and predictive analytics, digital platforms can identify patterns in how people think, react, and make choices. By studying past behavior, these systems can anticipate future preferences with remarkable accuracy. This predictive capability enables platforms to deliver personalized content, targeted advertisements, and customized recommendations designed to maintain user engagement.

Algorithms serve as the invisible architects of the digital experience. They determine which posts appear in social media feeds, which videos are recommended next, and which search results are displayed first. While these systems are designed to help users navigate the overwhelming volume of information available online, they also shape the pathways through which information flows. As a result, algorithms influence not only what people see but also how they interpret events and ideas.

Engineering of engagement has become a defining feature of modern digital platforms. Features such as infinite scrolling, personalized recommendations, and notification systems are carefully designed to encourage continuous interaction. Psychological principles—such as curiosity, social validation, and variable rewards—are embedded within these designs to sustain user interest. By understanding human behavior and emotional triggers, platforms create digital environments that feel immersive and difficult to leave.

Social media has amplified these dynamics by connecting billions of individuals within shared digital spaces. Posts, videos, and messages can spread rapidly through networks, reaching audiences that extend far beyond the original creator's circle. Viral content illustrates how emotional reactions and algorithmic amplification combine to determine which ideas receive widespread attention. Material that provokes strong emotional responses often travels further and faster than neutral information.

While these systems provide many benefits—such as easier access to information, new forms of communication, and opportunities for creativity—they also raise important questions about the balance between technology and human autonomy. When algorithms determine what information is prioritized, individuals may unknowingly encounter a curated version of reality shaped by engagement-driven systems. This dynamic can influence how opinions are formed, how discussions unfold, and how societies understand complex issues.

Another significant theme explored in this book is the increasing role of artificial intelligence in predicting and guiding human decisions. From recommending entertainment to influencing consumer purchases and assisting professional judgments, AI systems have become active participants in decision-making processes. Although these technologies often improve efficiency and convenience, they also highlight the growing influence of machine intelligence in everyday life.

Recognizing these dynamics does not mean rejecting digital

technologies or the innovations they bring. Instead, it encourages a deeper awareness of how these systems operate. Understanding the mechanisms behind algorithms, engagement strategies, and behavioral prediction allows individuals to interact with technology more consciously and critically.

Awareness is an important step toward maintaining control over personal attention and decision-making. When users understand how infinite feeds encourage prolonged scrolling, how notifications trigger habitual responses, and how emotional content spreads through networks, they gain the ability to evaluate their digital interactions more thoughtfully. Rather than being passive participants in algorithmically shaped environments, individuals can become more deliberate in how they consume information and engage with online platforms.

The future of artificial intelligence and digital platforms will likely bring even greater sophistication in how systems analyze and influence human behavior. Advances in machine learning, data analytics, and behavioral modeling will continue to expand the capabilities of technology. At the same time, societies will face ongoing challenges related to privacy, transparency, ethical design, and the preservation of independent thought.

Ultimately, the relationship between humans and intelligent machines is still evolving. The technologies that shape attention today will continue to develop, and the choices made by designers, policymakers, and users will determine how these systems influence society. By understanding the forces at work within the digital ecosystem, individuals and communities can participate more actively in shaping a technological future that supports knowledge, creativity, and human well-being.

The story of artificial intelligence, algorithms, and human attention is not simply a technological narrative, it is also a reflection of how societies adapt to new forms of influence and communication. In recognizing both the power and the responsibility that accompany these technologies, humanity can strive to ensure that innovation serves not only efficiency and engagement but also the deeper goals of understanding, autonomy, and meaningful connection in the digital age.

www.ingramcontent.com/pod-product-compliance
Lightning Source LLC
Chambersburg PA
CBHW041300210926
51847CB00009B/89

* 9 7 8 9 6 9 9 7 9 7 8 7 3 *